# PILLARS OF JUSTICE
the homeowner's guide to the law

# PILLARS OF JUSTICE

## JUSTICE

### the homeowner's guide to the law

Duncan Callow
LL.B Barrister

Otter Publications
Chichester, England

First published in 1996 by **Otter Publications**, 5 Mosse Gardens, Fishbourne, Chichester, West Sussex, PO19 3PQ.

**DISCLAIMER**
**Whilst the information herein is supplied in good faith, no responsibility is taken by either the publisher or the author for any damage, injury or loss, however caused, which may arise fro the use of the information provided.**

The male pronoun has been used throughout the book. This is simply to avoid ugly and cumbersome language, and no discrimination or bias is intended.

**British Library Cataloging in Publication Data**
A CIP record for this book is available through the British Library.
**ISBN** 1 899053 03 4

**Acknowledgements**
Again, I must express my sincere gratitude to Elaine Austin for putting in so many unsociable hours in typing an often indecipherable manuscript. I would also like to thank the Environmental Health Department at the London Borough of Sutton for their assistance with Chapter 7.

**Text design** by Angela Hutchings.
**Cover design** by Jim Wilkie.
**All cartoons** by Simon Golding.
**Printed and bound** in Great Britain by The Cromwell Press, through MBC.
**Distributed** in the UK by Plymbridge Distributors Ltd., Plymbridge House, Estover Road, Plymouth, PL6 7PZ.
*The Otter Publications logo is reproduced from original artwork by David Kitt.*

# Contents

# Introduction

From our late teens onwards, many of us have been encouraged to get onto the property ladder and watch our investments grow. Successive governments have made owning a property ever easier and lenders have been positively generous in advancing mortgage funds - but at a price. During the late 1980's and early 1990's the bubble finally burst on the housing market. Properties which had previously seen continual growth in their values suddenly became very difficult to sell. The investment benefit of bricks and mortar was brought into question. For the first time the problem which we now know as negative equity reared its ugly head. Many of these problems still pervade the UK's housing scene. The market has stagnated and the number of homes exchanged has fallen to an all-time low. Depressing news?

For some certainly. But times have changed and now more than ever a property should be viewed as a home and not as a short-term investment. I have therefore written this book for "home-owners" and not property speculators. It should be seen as a guide through the many legal aspects of purchasing, owning and running a home. Many will be well-known but many may come as something of a surprise. Given that a home will be the most expensive purchase of our lives, a working knowledge of the law as it affects us is critical. What are the steps to be taken in buying a house? Do you need planning permission to add a conservatory? How do you deal with noisy neighbours? How do you complain effectively about tradesmen or professionals? How much force can you use to restrain an intruder?

These may all be familiar questions, but knowing where to look for an answer has traditionally been a problem for the home-owner. I have drawn on many experiences in writing this book - some personal and many professional. I hope that you find Pillars of Justice informative and easy to read. It's been a fun project to work on and I hope that some of my enthusiasm has found its way on to the page.

The law is stated as at 1st August 1995. At the time of publication, it is expected that the small claims court threshold will have risen to £3000. Enjoy your home.

**Duncan Callow, Surrey.**

# Chapter 1

## The legal aspects of property ownership

As a nation, the ownership of property has become something of an obsession. Fuelled by central government policy, the greed culture of the late 1980's and a tidal wave of feel-good factor, home ownership is now at an all-time high. In Great Britain there are now 22 million households of which 64% are owner-occupied. In France, the situation is very different. The desire to own property has been displaced by a rather more practical approach to renting. Why be saddled with a twenty-five year mortgage and all the associated insecurities, when you can rent a home?

But there is undoubtedly a great deal of pride to be derived from home-ownership and a sense of satisfaction when the last mortgage payment is made. Every brick, every blade of grass and every potential problem owned outright! Getting the correct balance between what we can sensibly afford and the dream home is notoriously difficult. During recent years the economic recession has effectively stagnated the property market and caught out homeowners, insurers and financial institutions alike. Homeowners, who are caught in the relatively new net which is called negative equity (where the value of their property, even if they could sell it, is less than the money which they owe by way of mortgage), insurers, who originally offered policies which covered the shortfall in the market value after the property had been repossessed and the banks and building societies who suffered massively from bad debts. Not surprisingly, the latter two groups have now regrouped and taken steps to avoid such future losses. The homeowners conversely are still stuck in the negative equity trap. The victims are typically those who were first-time buyers during the last five years and who should now be moving on and providing an impetus to the whole cycle of property development and exchange.

But the news is not all gloomy. Many financial institutions do now offer varying degrees of rescue assistance and government is considering legislative change to reduce some of the burden. A basic understanding of land law and how property is held is essential for the well-informed homeowner. It is not an easy subject to understand and is fraught with pitfalls and complexities. Buying or renting a house whether outright or with the assistance of a mortgage is quite unlike any other purchase transaction. Regrettably people seldom own a simple parcel of land, the airspace above it and the soil beneath it. Unlike a new car or a pair of socks, land (or real property), will never wear out. There are very strong arguments which persistently call for an overhaul of the procedure for buying and selling land. Indeed, in spite of the historical problems and the rights which various parties may assert over land, in Scotland, the process is much simpler and more user-friendly. The Scottish system will be considered in a little more detail later, but for now the following aspects and definitions of land law will be considered.

## 1.1 REGISTERED LAND

It may be surprising that the bulk of property legislation dates back to 1925. The Law of Property Act 1925 and the Land Registration Act 1925 paved the way for a new and revolutionary system of land exchange. But until recently two rather haphazard systems ran in parallel - one for unregistered land and one for registered land. Under the former system where title (ownership) to property (land, buildings etc.) is unregistered, ownership is proven through a series of deeds. These are often cumbersome documents, bound with legal tape. With older properties particularly, they can make for fascinating reading as the whole history of the property is contained in each deed.

| Action | TITLE Unregistered | TITLE Registered |
|---|---|---|
| Seller prepares draft contract. Approved by buyers | | |
| Pre-contract enquiries and some searches by buyers | | |
| Exchange of contracts - usually with a deposit (5 or 10%) | | |
| Buyer insures property | | |
| Seller proves that he is the legal owner and can sell according to contract terms | Proved by inspection of the deeds giving legal ownership to the seller | Seller gives buyer an office copy of entries on the register |
| Buyer prepares purchase deed | Conveyance | Transfer |
| Pre-completion search by buyer | A check of Land Charges Registry | A check at the District Land Registry |
| Completion | Title deeds and conveyance to buyer on receipt of the balance of the purchase price. Legal estate passes | Land Certificate and transfer to buyer. Equitable interest posted |
| After completion | Conveyance stamped. First registration of title | Transfer stamped. Land Certificate and transfer lodged at the Land Registry for registration |

**Table 1. Buying a property - the legal steps.**

Details of owners, dates of sale and enforcement of covenants and easements (see later) can all be found. But by the same token, because each facet of ownership of the property requires a new deed, there was and still is, scope for lost papers and documents and for defects in title (i.e. less than 100% vacant possession) to creep in. For solicitors, unregistered land conveyancing has always been something of a risky business.

England and Wales is now subject to compulsory first registration. This means that in time only one system will apply, the simpler one for registered land. Those homes and parcels of land which are still unregistered (often those which have remained in the same family for many years) will have to be registered at the District Land Registry when a disposition of the property occurs. This means that as these homes are sold or otherwise disposed of, the buyer or his solicitor must register the title. In the past, where these pockets existed, a fresh investigation of title usually going back over at least 15 years had to be made.

Under the "new" system, administered by the Land Registry, title, i.e. proper ownership, is effectively guaranteed by the State. This means that the previous risks associated with the "old" system should, in theory at least, have largely dissipated. For solicitors and licensed conveyancers, provided they have not been negligent, mistakes and omissions by the Land Registry can be compensated for.

Once registered all details about title are entered onto the register. This is the registered owner's proof of title and he receives an official copy called a Land Certificate if the property is owned outright. If as is more likely, the property was bought with the assistance of a mortgage, then the lender is issued with a Charge Certificate (a mortgage being a type of legal charge) whilst the land certificate is retained by the Land Registry.

In a sense the register is similar to a vehicle registration document (V5) in that it details dates of transfer and first registration etc. A simple examination of both documents reveals much useful detail. However, like the V5, the register is not a complete record of all matters which affect the registered property. With the V5, only the registered legal keeper is recorded. This may not be the actual owner or the person who drives the car on a daily basis. So too with the register - in theory if the buyer does not make a careful, physical inspection of the property before purchase, he may take it subject to overriding interests which are not shown on any papers.

## Overriding interests

There are twelve overriding interests found in the Land Registration Act 1925. They are effectively third party rights or interests which will bind, i.e. override the interests of the buyer. The theory behind them is that they should be easily discovered from a physical inspection of the property. Overriding interests is a very fertile area of the law because many buyers have not purchased quite what they were expecting. With land and property being so expensive and such a personal matter, buyers have had no choice but to enter into costly litigation. The twelve overriding interests are:

1. Rights of common, drainage rights, customary rights, public rights, profits a prendre, rights of sheepwalk(!), rights of way, watercourses, rights of water.
2. Liability to repair highways by reason of tenure, quit-rents, crown rents.
3. Liability to repair the chancel of any church.
4. Liability in respect of embankments, and sea and river walls.
5. Payments in lieu of title and charges or annuities payable for the redemption of title rent charges.
6. Rights acquired or in the course of being acquired under the Limitation Acts.
7. The rights of every person in *actual occupation* of land or in receipt of the rents and profits thereof, except where enquiry is made of such person and the rights are not disclosed.
8. In the case of a possessory qualified or good leasehold title, all estates, rights, interests and powers excepted from the effect of registration.
9. Rights under local land charges unless and until registered or protected on the register in the prescribed form.
10. Rights of fishing and sporting, seigniorial and manorial rights of all descriptions.
11. Leases granted for a term of less than twenty-one years.
12. In respect of land registered before the commencement of the Land Registration Act 1925, rights to mines and minerals ...etc.

To the lay homeowner or prospective house buyer this probably looks like nothing more than legal jargon. True, many of the terms are now rather antiquated and are unlikely to have much application to a 1990's house-buying transaction. However, whether a DIY conveyancer or if using a solicitor, you must look out for several of the most important overriding interests. This is particularly so if you are using a solicitor who may seldom make a physical inspection of the property (because conveyancing fees are now so competitive, trips hither and thither out of the office would easily wipe out an already squeezed profit margin). Informal rights of way, leases under twenty-one years, squatters' rights and especially the rights of people in actual occupation, must be considered very carefully. Perhaps an example of an overriding interest may help:

Richard buys a large detached family home from Jonathan. At the bottom of the garden is a small granny annexe which is sold as part of the overall transaction. The day after Richard has been registered with title, he discovers Angela living in the annexe. She claims to have been paying rent to Jonathan for the last two years under an agreement that she could live in the annexe for four years. The question is whether this agreement is binding on Richard, i.e. does he have to let Angela stay in possession for the next two years? Because the purported lease is for less than twenty-one years, it need not have been registered and may take effect as an overriding interest against Richard. If the lease agreement was in writing (but not in a formal deed) it may be an equitable minor interest. But in any event Angela is probably a person with a proprietary interest (the lessee in actual occupation at the time the property was bought).

In simple terms this means that because a physical inspection of the property was not made prior to purchase, Angela has an overriding interest against Richard. He must let her stay for the duration of the lease.

## 1.2 UNREGISTERED LAND

Since compulsory first registration became effective at the end of 1990, the bulk of problems which face homeowners in respect of unregistered title have been concerned with enforceability of other interests. As already mentioned, when land is unregistered, ownership of it is found from title deeds rather than the land register. Under the system for dealing with unregistered land, leases and other overriding interests as seen above, have their own procedure for registration under the Land Charges Act 1972. Either the interest, such as a restrictive covenant, is registered on the Land Certificate, or it is void.

But as is so often the case, there are exceptions to this rule. There is a small class of rights which for some unknown reason are effectively non-registrable. However, they may still be binding on a new purchaser if he is "the bona fide purchaser of a legal estate for value without notice of this interest". This is where it all gets rather confusing and conceptually difficult for lawyers and lay people alike. But it is an important concept, so here is another example:

Richard and Judy are unmarried but have been living together in an unregistered house for the past 15 years. Although the house is in Richard's name, Judy has paid half of all the bills (including the mortgage repayments) since they started co-habiting. The relationship has broken down, so Richard puts the property on the market. **Murray is a keen potential buyer and instructs his solicitor to search the deeds to check that Richard has a good title and can sell the property on to him. Judy will probably have an equitable interest which under the old system was unregisterable. If Murray buys without notice of her interest (i.e. joint-occupation) then Judy's position will be protected.** Murray will be able to plead an absence of notice of her occupation only if he has made all the usual and proper enquiries and still found nothing to indicate her equitable interest. If he fell short of this standard he could not plead that he had no notice of rights which proper diligence ought to have discovered. Of such rights, Murray would have constructive notice and would therefore be bound by Judy's interest if he;

* had actual notice of some problem and a proper search would have defined it.
* deliberately failed to make proper enquiries to prevent him having notice of it.
* failed due to carelessness to make such enquiries that a buyer ought to make acting on his solicitor's advice!

As previously stated, all of England and Wales is now subject to compulsory first registration of title. If you are unsure whether your house has previously been registered, a simple call to your mortgagee (lenders) will shed some light. If they hold a Charge Certificate, then the property has been registered, and in theory at least, you may be able to conduct your own conveyancing (see Chapter 2). The following are some situations where you must always use a solicitor or licensed conveyancer:

* buying a council house.
* if parts of the house which you are buying are let to sitting tenants.
* newly-built houses. This is particularly important as it will be necessary for the solicitor to check that all of the boundaries have been properly drawn and what your rights may be in respect of certain easements and restrictive covenants etc.

## 1.3 EASEMENTS

In addition to certain rights over your own property, you may have rights in respect of other people's property. This right or easement, may come as part and parcel of your purchase or it may arise from a private agreement with the other property owner. An easement can properly be defined as a right enjoyed by one landowner over the land of another. Examples include rights of way, rights of light, rights of support and rights to air or water. The landowner who reaps the benefit of the easement is called the **dominant tenement** whilst the land over which the right is enjoyed is called the **servient tenement**. Further, a positive easement is a right to do something on the land of another (perhaps to cut wood) whilst a negative easement restricts the use the owner of the servient tenement may make of his land (perhaps restricting use of a right of way). Many easements are obvious and need not be laid down in tablets of stone. If you live on the first floor of a block of flats, you will buy it with an easement of support, i.e. that the flat underneath cannot effectively be demolished leaving you with nothing but fresh air for support! Although the owner of a servient tenement can be required to refrain from doing something, he cannot be required to physically do anything (apart from one exception - it may be a requirement to keep a fence in good order).

**Legal requirements of an easement**
• there must be dominant and servient land.
• the land must be owned by different people.
• the easement must relate to the "reasonable enjoyment" of the land and not the people who may be there at the time.

This latter requirement has given rise to a fair body of case-law and in many respects is therefore the most important. What is reasonable enjoyment is very much a question of fact according to the particular circumstances of the case but as a rule, judges will be cautious and consider whether the right is actually more significant than a mere transitory right. There is much confusion over rights to light. Is there such a thing? What if your neighbour plans an extension to his house and you think that your uninterrupted view of his garden will be obstructed? Do you have a God-given right to this light? Probably not. You could oppose his planning application on several grounds (see Chapter 4) but ancient rights to light are unlikely to be one of them. Easements (including light) are created in one of four main ways:

• by an Act of Parliament.
• by implied grant, for example you may sell a piece of land which you had previously used for access to your home. You may sell the land with an implied right of way.
• by express grant. Where you "buy" an easement from your neighbour having carefully considered all the paperwork, usually with the help of a solicitor.

* by prescription. Again this may be a somewhat contentious area as an easement can exist simply by virtue of the fact that the owners of the dominant tenement have for a long time (twenty years) enjoyed the right over the servient tenement without interruption.

Returning to the ancient lights example, it is clear that unless twenty uninterrupted years have lapsed, you may have problems attempting to enforce such an easement. Moreover, the acquisition of a prescriptive right to light may have been prevented by the registration of a local land charge (if in doubt, again seek legal advice).

**Disputes/enforcing an easement**
Because of their somewhat intangible nature, identifying and deriving the benefit of an easement can be a rather tricky exercise. Neighbour disputes are a notorious area and warrant an entire chapter to themselves (see Chapter 7) but they are often centred on a right of way or other easement. If your solicitor did his job properly at the outset then his enquiries should have considered the question of any easements. If alarm bells are set ringing then he ought to make further enquiries. However, conveyancing being the cut-throat business which it is today, there is clearly scope for error and it may come as something of a nasty shock to new purchasers of servient tenements when their neighbours seek to exercise their rights over your land. There is absolutely no point in asserting rights, or denying their existence until you have all the facts.

Neighbour disputes have a rather too familiar habit of developing and deteriorating because of personality clashes. In spite of your feelings at what may be a rather emotional time, you must not continue on a point of principle. You will fail. You cannot change your neighbours. If at all possible, try to resolve the dispute amicably and sensibly by looking at the paperwork which you have available. A search at the local Land Registry may prove to be of benefit. If the sensible approach fails or it seems that both parties have a meritorious claim, then it will doubtless have to be referred to solicitors, and possibly a barrister, for an expert opinion. This is where things get expensive especially as Legal Aid is unlikely to be available. An early resolution of any problems is therefore desirable and if not attained it is unlikely that you will have the knowledge or the ability to fight or defend your own claim. Disputes of this nature usually end up in the Lands Tribunal (see Useful Addresses) being played out between experienced barristers (counsel). Unlike industrial tribunals or the small claims procedure of the county court, the Lands Tribunal is very formal and not the arena for lay advocates.

## *1.4* COVENANTS

Most people tend to think of covenants in a purely restrictive capacity. For example there may be a covenant which affects your property by restricting the height of your conifers to four metres. But equally there may be mandatory or positive covenants which actually compel you to carry out certain functions, for example to empty the rubbish etc. Covenants generally are quite different from easements in that they are not actually part of the property bought or sold, but are simply agreements between two people. Many employees are familiar with the concept of restrictive covenants in their employment contracts. On a purely contractual basis between employer and employee, the latter may agree not to work for a competitor for twelve months following the termination of the existing contract. So too the situation in property law terms. Covenants are an important feature of property law generally. Here is an example which may clarify the situation a little.

> **Lord Snott is a landowner. Faced with crippling death duties he must sell some of his property to a developer but anxious not to spoil the rural nature of the area in its entirety, places a covenant in the sale deeds preventing more than 100 houses being built and insisting only on local stone being used in their construction. Twaing Plc accepts the purchase on these terms - if it didn't like them, it could simply walk away and buy land for development elsewhere. But Twaing Plc also places covenants in the sale of each home to the new purchasers. In particular a covenant prohibits the erection of satellite dishes and compels all homeowners not to grow hedges above one and a half metres. In both cases, these restrictions are made in the form of written covenants set out in the deed. Again, the purchasers will be fully aware (or ought to be made aware by their solicitors) so that if they are keen to watch satellite TV they ought to check the availability of a cable supply instead.**

Although the covenants originally bind the two parties to the agreement, it is usually the intention of the covenantor (the landowner who creates the covenant), that they bind all subsequent owners of the property. Again, cases have gone through the courts on the question of enforceability of restrictive covenants and just how many successors in title (new owners) are to be bound. As a general rule it seems that all new buyers should always assume that the covenants found on the register can be enforced.

**Enforcement and passage of time**
Covenants are often beneficial in binding all the homeowners in a particular area so that everyone lives by a uniform set of rules. But returning to our earlier example, it is highly probable that one or several of the new buyers would openly erect a satellite dish. Who would or should enforce the covenant? The developer introduced the covenant for the benefit of all the people on the estate so if they took umbridge at those who flouted it, then they would have to lobby Twaing Plc and eventually threaten proceedings. In practice it is more likely that the covenant would not be enforced and would drift into oblivion.

With each new owner, there is no direct contractual relationship (privity of contract) with the original covenantor. But the general rules relating to enforcement do not require privity of contract between plaintiff and defendant. This is usually the case in disputes between freeholders but may also occur between a landlord and a tenant (leaseholder). Covenants contained in a lease agreement may include obligations to insure and keep the property in good order. The burden of these covenants will bind any subsequent tenant.

To be enforceable, a covenant must "touch and concern" the land in question. If it does then it is possible for the benefit to pass as either a legal or equitable right. Under the former, the remedy for a breach of covenant is damages, i.e. financial compensation. Under equitable principles you could seek an injunction for breach of a restrictive covenant and an order for specific performance (compelling the other party to carry out the requirement of the covenant) where a positive (or mandatory) covenant has been breached.

Many covenants date back many years and were created at a time of very different attitudes and social tastes. They may have no relevance to the property owner of today. If this is the case, the covenant is unlikely to be enforceable, or if it is, you can apply through a solicitor to have its effect nullified.

## 1.5 PUBLIC RIGHTS OF WAY

Given the increased amount of leisure time which we are all supposed to have today, it is perhaps no surprise that many people seek their recreation out in the open air. Come rain or shine, ramblers, orienteers, mountain bikers etc. will take to the hills clad in shiny lycra and state of the art footwear. All of us at some stage will have enjoyed a rather less energetic and perhaps sartorially more conservative, stroll on a Summer's afternoon. But where do we wander? As a reader this may be all rather too close to home if you are faced with "visitors" to your property asserting a public right of way across your manicured lawn. It is an emotive issue and one which has received considerable media coverage. Just where should the lines be drawn?

One important point to note is that even on common land i.e. not privately owned, there is no absolute right of access for members of the public to use and abuse. Of course, public footpaths and bridleways are open for all to use although the landowners or farmers may be equally as guilty of spoiling the picture. Planting crops or rerouting paths have been used in the past as tactics to lead the populace astray. However, a thought ought to be spared for landowners (whilst not actually condoning their action) when the damage that we are all capable of causing is considered. Boots, bikes, dogs and litter can all leave expensive scars on the landscape.

If you are the landowner then you can apply to have the footpath rerouted. To do so will need the approval of other interested parties and probably your local authority. If the footpath is simply never used then you could also apply to have its use as a right of way extinguished altogether. But this is not as easy as it sounds. Because one of the formalities which has to be complied with is the advertisement of your application, walkers will soon cotton on and use the footpath thereby knocking your application out for the count.

We are probably all aware that, *"Trespassers Will Be Prosecuted"*. In fact, this is a nonsense. Although we may be entitled to use a public footpath, if we stray from it, a trespass will have been committed. But this is not a criminal offence which can be prosecuted. The owner's only remedy would be to claim damages for the fact that you have trodden on his adjoining land. Quantifying the loss is almost impossible and likely to amount to a few pence at best (see Chapter 7). Here is an example of the possible problems associated with a public footpath and how easily they can be removed.

**Barry and Elaine live in a small village in Rutland. They have a large garden with a top quality tennis court for their son Paul who is a budding star of the future. The bad news is that a public right of way intersects the garden between their conservatory and the tennis court. This rather stifles Barry's pleasure which is playing tennis in the nude. Barry is then posted overseas so the house is put on the market. It is a lovely home but fails to reach its true market value because of the right of way. Jim and Sarah, the new owners are not put off however and make an application to reroute the path to the bottom of the garden behind a small stand of pine trees. The application sails through unopposed with the locals apparently quite relieved that they no longer have to invade anybody's privacy. Barry is still searching for the ultimate privacy to indulge his fantasy ...**

## 1.6  TENURE

Tenure is the rather ancient term used to describe how property is held. It dates back to the feudal system of landholding and for our purposes encompasses freehold, where no service is required of the owner for the use of the land, and leasehold tenure. Generally houses are held on a freehold and flats on a leasehold.

### Freehold

The full term is "a legal estate in fee simple". It is the most complete form of ownership in land. If you own the freehold to your property then in theory at least, once the mortgage has been redeemed, you own every aspect of it absolutely in perpetuity (for ever).

### Leasehold

Many potential home owners are rather wary of the term leasehold because they feel that they will only be renting their home from the true owner for the duration of the lease. In a sense they never really *own* their home. Technically, they are probably correct because the leaseholder owns the property for a fixed period after which it reverts to the actual owner or freeholder. But in practical terms, buying a property subject to a long lease really is as good as a freehold especially given the protection afforded the leaseholder under the leasehold reform legislation (see later).

The principal raison d'etre for leaseholds is in respect of restrictive covenants between neighbouring leaseholders. For example, in a new development of  twenty flats it would be pointless issuing twenty freeholds. Given the communal nature of such a development, it is important that the freeholder should be able to enforce rights against each leaseholder and indeed that each leaseholder can enforce covenants against each other. Mutual repairing obligations are required between flat-owners and this can only happen between leaseholders. By way of example, the leaseholder of a second storey flat must be able to enforce covenants against the first floor and ground floor flats in respect of maintenance of his support - otherwise he would fall down. The way the law is currently drafted, this right only exists between leaseholders.

In a development of flats, the developer may hold onto the freehold (or itself the leasehold if it too has only been able to secure such tenure from the ultimate owner) or after a few years it may sell it onto a management company in which each leaseholder would have a stake. The management company will then administer and collect the annual service charge for things like communal lighting and heating, refuse collection and general maintenance. Each "shareholder", although not owning the freehold, will form part of the decision-making process in terms of the day-to-day running of their own flat. Many leaseholders become rather apathetic in practice, fail to turn up to annual meetings or to have any positive input throughout the year and then wonder why the management company has assumed ostensible control. It is important to take an interest and to question any proposals with which you are unhappy. The classic area for contention is in respect of the buildings insurance premium.

| VARIABLE | FREEHOLD | LEASEHOLD |
|---|---|---|
| Security of Tenure | Absolute unless - <br>(i) repossession by mortgagee <br>(ii) property compulsorily purchased | Absolute unless - <br>(i) repossession by mortgagee <br>(ii) property compulsorily purchased <br>(iii) eviction by freeholders in extreme cases where lease terms breached |
| Mortgage | Easy to obtain subject to lenders terms | Generally available provided sufficient of the lease still to run after mortgage paid off |
| Changes to property | Generally freeholder can do as he pleases subject to - <br>(i) local planning controls <br>(ii) restrictive covenants | May well be onerous terms in the lease preventing change |
| Insurance | Will be a requirement by the mortgagee to insure buildings adequately. No requirement to insure contents | Management company or other limited company will insure buildings from the annual service charge. Contents insurance at the discretion of leaseholder |
| Repairing Obligations | Unlikely | Likely particularly in respect of general upkeep |

Table 2. A summary of the principal differences between leasehold and freehold property.

### 1.7 LEASEHOLD REFORM
**Flats**
As already stated, many people have traditionally been wary of taking on a long lease because one day they know that their home will have to be returned to the freeholder. Moreover a lease with only a few years left to run may be a difficult proposition to sell.

Now, under the Leasehold Reform, Housing and Urban Development Act 1993 long leaseholders of flats have the right to buy the freehold if they buy as a group. This is referred to as the right to enfranchise and applies even if the freeholder does not wish to sell. This is a group right. On an individual basis, a leaseholder of a flat has the right to renew his lease for another ninety years on top of the existing lease. But there are qualifications:

- The lease must originally have been granted for more than twenty-one years. You do not have to be the first lessee.
- The lease must be at a low rent. This is calculated thus:

(i)  If the lease was granted before 1st April 1963, the rent due in the first year of the lease must have been not more than two-thirds of the letting value of your flat at the start of that year. You can ascertain the letting value of your lease by reference to a chartered surveyor.

(ii)  If the lease was granted on or between 1st April 1963 and 31st March 1990, the rent due in the first year of the lease must not have been more than two-thirds of the rateable value of your flat at the start of that year (your local authority will hold a list of rateable values).

or

(iii)  If the lease was granted on or between 1st April 1963 and 31st March 1990, but your flat did not have a rateable value at the start of the lease or at any time before 1st April 1990, the rent due in the first year of the lease must not have been more than £1000 in Greater London or £250 elsewhere.

or

(iv)  If the lease was granted on or after 1st April 1990, the rent due in the first year of the lease must not have been more than £1000 in Greater London or £250 elsewhere. Remember that the figure referred to is rent or ground rent. Do not confuse this with your annual mortgage repayment.

There are additional requirements in respect of residence. For enfranchisement (group purchase of the freehold) at least half of the tenants must have lived in their flats as their main home for the last twelve months or for periods that add up to three years in the last ten. On an individual lease renewal basis then you must have occupied your flat as your main home for at least the last three years or again for periods that add up to three years during the past ten. The building too must qualify for enfranchisement. There must be two or more flats and not more than 10% of the internal floor area can be used for non-residential (e.g. business) use. Also at least two-thirds of all the flats in your building must be let to qualifying tenants.

**Exceptions**
As always there have to be exceptions, so it is worth considering the following carefully. You cannot be a qualifying tenant if:

• your landlord is a charitable housing trust and the flat is provided by the charity.
• you own qualifying leases in more than two flats in the building.
• yours is a business lease.

In respect of the building, you cannot enfranchise or renew the lease if it:

• is within the precinct boundary of a cathedral.
• is built on certain National Trust land.
• is owned by the Crown.
• is a converted building of four or fewer flats and the freeholder has lived in one of the flats as his main residence for the last twelve months (this exception applies only to enfranchisement).
• has been given a conditional exemption from Inheritance Tax by the Inland Revenue.

*The process*
With both enfranchisement and lease renewal there is a set of procedures and notices which have to be followed closely. It is probably best to instruct a solicitor who is familiar with these processes and who can probably standardise the entire transaction. There can be problems. The parties may not be able to reach an agreement which may jeopardise the transaction as time limits have to be adhered to.

*The cost*
This may be the major stumbling block to your particular leasehold reform. Every case will turn on its own facts and for this reason alone it is impossible to say what the charges will be.
   But the price of the freehold or a lease renewal is based on three variable factors:

- open market value.
  Enfranchisement. The value of the interests held by all the landlords in the property.
  Lease renewal. The reduction in the value of the landlord's interest in your flat affected by the new lease.
- compensation to the landlord.
- half or more of the marriage value. This has nothing to do with wedlock but in enfranchisement means the additional value brought about by the freehold and leasehold interests being under the same control. In lease renewal there will be an increase in the value of the tenant's interest and a fall in the landlord's. There will usually be an overall increase in the total value of the two interests. The marriage value is the difference between the total value of the interests before and after lease renewal.

## Houses

The Leasehold Reform Act 1967 (as amended) allows homeowners with long leases to either purchase the freehold or to extend the lease by up to fifty years. Again, it is a very complicated piece of legislation and not one to which the term "user-friendly" could be readily applied. But it is of value and the following points should be considered:

- the Act only applies to houses. Because of this, there have been many questions raised about the definition of "house". It now seems that where a property has been divided vertically into separate dwellings, then the result is a house. Horizontal divisions means flats.
- the leaseholders must have lived in the house for the past three years.
- the lease must be a long lease (the same definition is used as for flats).
- if you are a qualifying leaseholder and wish to buy or extend then the freeholder cannot deny you your rights unless it is a public body with an identifiable need to develop the property within the next ten years. The only other exception may apply where the freeholder acquired the freehold prior to 1966 and he and his family have a greater need for the house than the leaseholder. But instances such as this will be rare.

### The cost

Again this may be the central issue and unfortunately there is no simple answer. In valuing the freehold the parties try to consider how much it would be worth with the tenant in occupation. This of course means that leaseholders will generally get a good buy if the lease only has a few years left to run. As a leaseholder, you will also have to pay the reasonable costs and expenses of the freeholder, for example legal and other professional fees.

## 1.8 SHARED OWNERSHIP
Leasehold and freehold have already been considered as forms of home ownership. Shared ownership is not widespread as it is only available to secure tenants - not tenants under assured shorthold or other private tenancy agreements. The concept is simple; a secure tenant buys a share in his or her flat from the landlord, say 75%. Because the landlord has retained a 25% interest in the property he will receive 25% of the proceeds of sale if the property is eventually sold.

## 1.9 RENTING
Renting privately and the implications for both the tenant and especially the landlord are considered in detail in Chapter 6. For now we are concerned with renting in the public arena, for example from the council or housing association. This type of household tenure still accounts for well over 25% of the total in Great Britain. In some notable areas the figure is considerably higher. Whilst this guide is intended primarily for owner-occupiers, the importance of non-private renting should not be underestimated. These types of "rent" are covered briefly.

### Housing Associations
These are non-profit making independent organisations which may have charitable purposes. Housing Associations are a popular form of tenure because they cater for many peoples' diverse needs. They also vary greatly in size and whilst many receive money from central and local government many too take on a more independent and businesslike role.

You will have to contact the housing department of your local authority to see whether any Associations are operating in your borough. Many associations take nominations from the local authority so consider whether this route is open to you. Otherwise contact the Association direct to ascertain their application procedure. The government body which regulates the Associations registered with it is called the Housing Corporation. Those that are registered are required by law to indicate their selection criteria and how the limited number of tenancies are allocated.

### Housing Co-operatives
A co-operative is another alternative to purely private housing and allows a greater degree of autonomy than renting from the local authority. A co-operative is a group of people who collectively own and manage their

housing. Ideally, co-ops are run democratically and on a non-hierarchical basis so that everyone has an equal say in how the housing is managed. Co-operatives are a relatively new concept in Great Britain but growing in popularity. To be truly successful they require a not inconsiderable commitment of time and energy on a purely voluntary basis. If this is forthcoming, then the benefits can be quite obvious, but the temptation to let the chores wait until another day may mean that they are of only limited success.

## Council housing

Different councils have different priorities for their housing stock. They all have a legal duty to find housing for those with priority needs (pregnant women, people with dependent children under sixteen, physically and mentally disabled, aged, those homeless because of an emergency) and who did not make themselves intentionally  homeless.

The local council is obliged to give you details of its allocation scheme and its application procedure. You should at least register on the council list even if it seems interminably long. Once on the list it may appear that you are treading water. Whether you make any progress up the list will depend upon the housing needs priorities of each local council. In general there are four ways in which the council will decide who goes to the top of the list and is offered housing:

- Points scheme.
- Group scheme.
- Date order scheme.
- Merit scheme.

Which scheme or combination of schemes that your council operates should be discussed with the relevant authority. Local Citizens' Advice Bureaux and Law Centres offer sound practical advice and tips on how to try to move more swiftly up the list. They may also help on questions of intentional homelessness. If the council decides that you have made yourself homeless on purpose when the accommodation you lived in was perfectly adequate or that you had been evicted for non-payment of rent, then your chances of obtaining council housing will have been severely diminished (to say the least!). But the council must act reasonably and consider all of the facts carefully to see if there is a genuine housing need. For example an eviction for non-payment of rent may have arisen because of an acute family problem. If you feel aggrieved at the council's interpretation of your situation, seek specialist advice on the appeals procedure.

## 1.10  JOINT OWNERSHIP

Buying a property is very often done on a joint basis. Any disposition of property can be fraught with problems and rather complex. There is scope for even greater confusion about conflicting interests if your home is bought other than by one person using one mortgage. There are two ways of buying and holding land on a joint basis; under a joint-tenancy or a tenancy in common. They are entirely different methods of holding property and the basic distinctions should be fully understood.

### Joint-tenancy

Under a joint-tenancy, each party owns the entire property as a whole. There are not separate shares available. There is one title which is owned in full by all the joint tenants. It is a state of concurrent ownership by at least two people although they are treated as one owner. For a valid joint-tenancy to exist there are four requirements:

- unity of possession - this means that each joint-tenant is entitled to possession of the entire property all of the time.
- unity of interest - each joint-tenant has the same interest in the property.
- unity of title - the interest in the property is derived from the same legal document.
- unity of time - each joint-tenant's interest takes effect in the property at the same time.

These four unities are not actually as difficult to unite as may often thought to be the case. If they are in existence, then the principal characteristic of a valid joint-tenancy is what happens on the death of one of the joint-tenants. Quite simply, the interest of the deceased passes automatically to the other joint-tenant. This is why in the case of most matrimonial homes owned on a joint basis, when one spouse dies the other inherits the deceased's share without the need for a formal document. This automatic transfer will defeat even any attempts which the deceased joint-tenant had made under a will to transfer his share. Therefore, even if the will says to the contrary, under a joint-tenancy, the property transfers automatically to the surviving joint-tenant(s).

### Tenancy in common

This is a quite different form of property ownership again by two or more people, because they have a distinct share in the property. There is only one of the four unities - unity of possession because each of the tenants in common owns an undivided share. If it often used by multiple purchasers or families. For example three cousins may each decide to buy a property with each contributing a third of the purchase price. Unlike a joint-tenancy they will all hold a separate share (in this case, one-third) of the property. It is also different because other survivorship rules apply. Under a tenancy in common, each tenant can deal with their share as they please, including under a will.

## Severance/termination of the joint-ownership

Problems have a familiar habit of occurring where property is held jointly. Relationships breakdown, circumstances change and people move on. If you buy a property on an equitable tenancy in common basis then your solicitor may well ask all the parties to sign an agreement which details the procedure to be followed if one of the tenants in common wants out. Remember that under a tenancy in common, each party holds an undivided share which is capable of realisation at any time. In the absence of such agreement, or if the other parties will not agree, then the party who wishes to sell can take the matter to court for an order severing the tenancy in common and sanctioning the sale. This is usually the last resort as the tenant who wants out could have sold his shares to the others or sold or otherwise transferred his interest to anyone.

Severing a joint-tenancy when each tenant holds the entire legal estate as distinct from a particular share, can be a simple conveyancing - type transaction using a solicitor. If the parties are not in agreement then it is another matter altogether and may ultimately end up in court for resolution. Below is an example of the type of agreement which tenants in common may sign prior to purchase. It clearly spells out each party's interest and obligations so that in the event of the relationship breaking down there *should* be no room for argument.

THIS DEED OF DECLARATION OF TRUST is made the 31st day of December 1995 BETWEEN DUNCAN ALEXANDER CALLOW of Buckingham Palace Mews, SW1X (hereinafter called "Mr Callow") on the one part and NAOMI HELENA CRAWFORD of 40 Pretty Faces Villas, London NW6 6XX (hereinafter called "Miss Crawford") on the other part both of whom are collectively called hereinafter "the Trustees".
WHEREAS:
(1)     The Trustees are the proprietors of the leasehold property known as Flat 5 on the second floor of 40 Pretty Faces Villas, London NW6 the title of which is registered at H M Land Registry under title number NGL6971.
(2)     The Trustees have agreed to declare the trusts upon which the said property is held in manner hereinafter appearing.
NOW THIS DEED WITNESSETH as follows
        In pursuance of the said agreement and in consideration of the premises the Trustees hereby agree and declare as follows:

1. The Trustees hold the said property on trust to sell, call in and convert the same into money with full power to postpone during such period as the Trustees shall think proper, sell in conversion of the same and to retain the same without being responsible for any loss occasioned thereby.

**2.** The Trustees hold the said property until sale an thereafter the net proceeds of sale upon trust in the shares described below.

**3.** If either of the Trustees wishes to sell his or her interest in the property then he or she will give the other trustee of trustees 3 months notice of intention to sell to expire no sooner than two years from the date the other trustee or trustees and the property shall be sold at a price to be agreed between them or in the absence of agreement at a price determined by an independent surveyor appointed by the Trustees.

**4.** Miss Crawford will be responsible for payment of all gas, electricity and telephone charges and for payment of all the instalments due under the mortgage to The Rip-off Bank Limited.

**5.** The Trustees shall be responsible in equal shares for the payment of the ground rent, buildings insurance, contents insurance, service charges, general and water rates and routine repairs, maintenance and decoration.

**6.** Miss Crawford will until the sale of the property as soon as reasonably possible after the date hereof take a paying lodger at the best payment for use and occupation reasonably obtainable and Mr Callow will be exclusively entitled to such income.

**7.** On a sale of the property the proceeds after deduction of estate agent's commission and any other incidental costs of sale shall be divided in equal shares between the Trustees and Miss Crawford will be solely responsible for redeeming the aforesaid mortgage out of her half share.

**8.** Any dispute about the construction of this agreement shall be referred to an independent arbitrator appointed by the Royal Institute of Chartered Surveyors whose decision shall be final and binding.

**IN WITNESS WHEREOF** the parties hereto have set their hands and seals the day and year first above written

**SIGNED SEALED AND DELIVERED**　　)
by the said DUNCAN ALEXANDER　　)
CALLOW in the presence of　　)

**SIGNED SEALED AND DELIVERED**　　)
by the said NAOMI HELENA　　)
CRAWFORD in the presence of　　)

## *1.11* MATRIMONIAL PROBLEMS

Disputes about property rights on marital breakdown are legend and seemingly it is only ever the lawyers who stand to benefit. This book is certainly no substitute for professional advice, nor an attempted thesis on the current state of our divorce laws. But given the record level of marital breakdown it is important to appreciate the sort of problems which can ensue if various interests are either not declared or not protected at the right time. Fighting to preserve your perception of your rights can be an extremely expensive, protracted and painful exercise. It is worth bearing in mind too that couples who agree to split on an amicable basis may soon be at each other's throats once lawyers become involved. Here is another practical example:

In 1993 Keith and Cindy buy their first home. The house was bought with the aid of a 95% mortgage, and the balance of 5% paid in cash by Keith. The house was conveyed solely into Keith's name as he was the principal breadwinner - a successful solicitor specialising in planning law. Cindy stays at home and runs parties selling female fashion accessories on a part-time basis. She uses her limited income to pay for luxuries and the occasional monthly mortgage repayment when Keith has a cash-flow problem. In August 1995 Keith wins a substantial prize on the National Lottery and uses nearly all of it to pay off the mortgage. However by the end of 1995 one of Keith's clients has sued him for £750,000 because he has been negligent. Keith has no indemnity insurance and is made bankrupt. The trustee in bankruptcy wants to sell the house to pay off some of Keith's debts. At first sight, Cindy seems to have no rights. When the house is purchased, Keith is the legal and equitable owner and there has been no declaration of trust giving Cindy any protection. However, it is possible for a non-legal owner to claim an equitable ownership interest in someone else's property provided she falls within one of the following categories:

* If Keith has made a clear promise to her that she should have an interest and she has relied on that promise to her detriment.
* If Cindy has contributed directly to the purchase price of the house, an interest may have arisen. Cindy's party planning does generate some income and whilst paying for luxuries is unimportant, her mortgage contributions, particularly at critical times may give her an equitable interest. Every case turns on its own facts and some further enquiries would have to be made of Cindy to ascertain the precise level of her contributions.

But if she has contributed sufficiently, then the property is co-owned. In legal terms, Keith would hold the legal estate for himself and the equitable estate on trust for himself  and Cindy as tenants in common. However, this is unlikely to protect Cindy indefinitely because Keith's legal estate in the house would be transferred to his trustee in bankruptcy. He could then apply to the court for an order for sale. Of course the court will not wish to turf Cindy out on the street and it must balance the competing interests. However Cindy has probably only a small interest in the property so a lengthy postponement of sale will be ordered. On sale her interest will have priority over the other creditors - i.e. the proceeds will settle her interest first. If Cindy is unable to establish an interest in the property then her final redress may be under the Matrimonial Homes Act 1983. But this only protects non-owning spouses by giving them a right of occupation if a notice is entered on the registered title.

The circumstances of this example may appear rather extreme, and to an extent they probably are. However the principles which underpin it are exactly the same, whatever your particular situation. They say love is blind so that at the start of a relationship couples probably will not wish to consider a breakdown, or the technicalities involved. Human nature. But when you're on your own, ask around and you may realise that careful planning at the outset could prove critical.

### 1.12 UNMARRIED FAMILIES

Many couples choose not to marry. Many couples cannot legally marry because they are gay or lesbian. Regrettably the law does not readily accept the unmarried family so on breakdown, establishing rights of ownership may prove almost impossible. The power to allocate matrimonial property on divorce simply does not extend to unmarried couples. If you therefore move in with another person and do not marry, in legal terms you are really only ever a lodger. If the relationship breaks down it is unlikely that you could claim an interest in that property in spite of years of washing-up, ironing, mowing the lawn etc. Only those tangible goods which you had brought into the relationship such as a TV, and which are capable of ready identification, can be "reclaimed". To protect your position, and if funds permit, consider buying into the property and holding as tenants in common. Such a proposal will soon highlight how keen the other party is on you! If in doubt speak with an experienced solicitor. If the property is held in joint names, the following principles should apply:

- the property will be divided in shares according to the intention of the parties or in complying with any agreement.
- such an intention or agreement may be in writing, agreed orally or inferred from conduct.

Your solicitor should therefore discuss your intentions and express each party's interest on the transfer documents or via a declaration of trust. Every transfer into joint names should contain a declaration of trust. The declaration should state whether the property is held as joint tenants or tenants in common and whether in equal or unequal shares. The declaration may also need to provide as to who is paying the mortgage and making the repairs etc.

# Chapter 2

## Buying a house (and selling!)

In Chapter 1 we saw an outline of how property is held and some of the associated problems. This chapter discusses the steps to be followed in buying (and selling) your house. It is not a DIY guide to conveyancing. With all of England and Wales now being subject to compulsory first registration of title, in theory there ought to be more scope for budding DIYers. However, if nothing else, Chapter 1 ought to have raised awareness of the pitfalls which await the unwary. Many people are competent enough to service their own cars and don't have to pay garage bills. But by the same token, if we have a tooth abscess, home extraction is not to be contemplated. But finding a good solicitor may prove problematic. There are good solicitors, bad solicitors and indifferent solicitors. The best are those who come recommended by friends and colleagues. Also, if you are buying with the aid of a mortgage, the lender (mortgagee) may be very reluctant to let you do it yourself. After all they are advancing big sums and will need to know that they are getting good security for their money. Rather, this chapter aims to break down some of the mysteries which surround household conveyancing. Buying a house is a very stressful time for all concerned, but for a busy high street firm of solicitors or licensed conveyancers, yours may be but one transaction amongst several hundred. For the lawyer, the steps to be followed will be taken for granted and he may not have the time nor desire to explain everything to you in minute detail.

## Background

Two-thirds of Britons own their homes, which is a much higher proportion than in continental Europe. This obsession with owning and not renting has acted as a catalyst for inflation. In the 1980's artificially high house prices led consumers to believe in their own wealth. Saving dropped off and we were all encouraged to borrow more and more. Not only to take on bigger mortgages but also to fit out these wonderful homes with new carpets, kitchens, bathrooms etc. It is arguable that the house price booms of the 1980's will never be witnessed again. The slump (which in some cases has seen property prices fall by over 30%) has left almost two million people in the negative equity net. Mortgagees have naturally taken a keen interest in stopping the rot. Mortgage arrears are still rising, house prices falling (increasingly slowly in some areas) and the number of homes exchanged sunk to around 1 million (average 1.7 million in the 1980's) per annum.

But it is not all bad news for everyone. Lower prices for first-time buyers are of course good news and many homeowners looking to trade-up, can do so and get better value for money. The emphasis now should clearly be on a house as a home and not as a speculative investment. In the long-term this may be no bad thing if inflationary pressures are kept under control and house prices not subjected to cyclical boom and bust periods. In Germany as in France, where there is a much higher proportion of good private sector rented accommodation, the economy has sustained steady growth and without high inflation. This is undoubtedly due in part to a different attitude to home ownership.

## 2.1 BUYING

The basic steps are:

- choose your home - the criteria you apply will vary according to many factors, but it is always worth remembering that you can always change the look of your home internally and externally (subject to planning controls) but you can **NEVER** change its location.
- ascertain how much you can afford. You should have already spoken with several lenders and got the provisional go-ahead.
- make the offer to the estate agent. It may add weight to your commitment if this is in writing. The estate agent may also request a returnable goodwill deposit of say £250. This is not a legal requirement and does not mean that you are locked into a purchase, but it may tip the balance in your favour.
- instruct a surveyor.
- instruct a solicitor/licensed conveyancer. Again, go with one personally recommended to you.

The solicitor will then:

(i) Write to all the relevant parties and obtain a local search. The local search is carried out at the local authority and is intended to reveal any aspects such as sewers and road building schemes which may affect your intended property. It is an important search and helps the solicitor in assimilating all the relevant information. If you are in any doubt about future development you must raise these with your solicitor. The local authority is only obligated to answer those questions which your solicitor raises. If your solicitor is therefore unaware, it may be too late to do anything about it. Local searches are not flawless and only as good as the information available at the time the search is made. It may be that your neighbour puts in a planning application to build a private airfield in his garden the day that you complete your purchase. This is always a risk.

Local searches can in some instances take an interminably long time to come back. This is not because your proposed property is subject to an endless list of problems, but because the local authority is understaffed. You can speed things up. You can either attend your local searches department and do the work yourself, or pay a premium fee to your solicitor to arrange for one of his junior staff to carry out the search in person. This may be money well spent if you are in a race to exchange contracts.

(ii)  Liaise with the mortgage lender to ensure that a mortgage offer will be forthcoming.

(iii)  Check that your survey is satisfactory.

(iv)  Approve the draft contract of sale prepared by the vendor's solicitor. The draft contract will be amended by both solicitors until both parties are happy and all the legal T's crossed and I's dotted.

(v)  A form of enquiries will also be sent to the vendor. This is a quite detailed questionnaire further intended to ensure that there is no confusion as to what the buyer is purchasing and the vendor selling. In particular, the question of fixtures and fittings will be raised. This opportunity should be used widely. You can basically ask any question you like although much of the form of enquiries will take on a standard form. If you are in any doubt at all about anything, speak with your solicitor. Better to make a nuisance of yourself at this stage than to be burdened with a problem after you move in.

(vi)  Check that the vendor has a good title to the property and can therefore legally sell it on to you. This search is carried out at the Land Registry. After the searches have come back and all appears to be acceptable, the mortgage offer is on the table and the survey reveals no particular problem, your solicitor draws up the contract of purchase in the form agreed by both sides. Two copies are prepared - one for the buyer and one for the seller.

**Exchange of contracts**
Three very important words conveying the legal title to a property to the purchaser. The respective solicitors will agree a date for completion, usually four weeks after exchange and then, often by telephone, a synchronised exchange will take place. Each solicitor will then send to the other the contract. In the case of a purchase a deposit of 5 or 10% will also usually be required. This is the critical stage in any property transaction and for the purchaser, takes on immense significance. On exchange, the legal title is vested in the purchaser. He cannot back out without expecting to face severe consequences. If you cannot complete the deal, the vendor may be advised to seek an order for specific performance compelling you to go ahead, or else to seek substantial damages for breach of contract, including forfeiture of the

deposit. It is therefore absolutely crucial to ensure that you have the funds and the desire to complete the transaction. Because legal title is vested in the purchaser, it is then his responsibility to insure the buildings.

## Completion

At this stage the balance of the purchase price is paid by your solicitor (he having received the mortgage advance from the mortgagee). The equitable title is then vested and the property is yours! Congratulations. Delays in completion are not uncommon and this should not be confused with a *failure* to complete. If the buyer causes the delay he may have to pay interest on the money owed to the vendor. The solicitor acting for the vendor may also be forced to issue a completion notice compelling the purchaser to complete within a specified time. If the vendor has caused the delay then the purchaser can cancel the contract and seek a refund of his deposit. He will more likely sue for breach of contract and claim damages for the losses he has sustained.

## Post completion formalities

### Stamp duty

1% of the total price for purchases over £60,000. This does not mean that the first £60,000 is exempt, so if you buy a house of £101,000 the Stamp Duty will be £1,090. If you pay £59,995, then no Stamp Duty at all is payable. If you have agreed to take on several fixtures and fittings and say the cooker, you should treat these as a separate contract. If for example the purchase price is £59,995 and the agreed figure for fixtures and fittings is a further £2,000, this would take you over the threshold and into Stamp Duty dues. Again, be guided by your solicitor.

### Registration of your interest at the Land Registry

A fee will be payable for the privilege!

## 2.2 FURTHER DETAIL

### Mortgages

Very few of us are fortunate to be able to buy outright. How much you can afford, and more importantly how much the mortgagee is prepared to lend, therefore plays an important part in the conveyancing transaction. Each lender has a different policy on home loans lending. 100% mortgages are now less readily available and the most you will be able to borrow is 95% of the purchase price or valuation. For a remortgage, this figure may be reduced to around 80%. If you can find an institution which is prepared to offer 100%, expect to pay a premium because of the greater risk involved. If you are a first-time buyer, the lender may offer an array of tempting carrots. Lenders, especially building societies, have had a tough time in attracting enough new borrowers so may well offer fixed rates, cash rebates and free legal and other professional fees.

## How much can you borrow?

Again this depends upon the policy of the lender but generally, multiply your annual income by 3. This can cause problems for sales-people or others who work on commission unless the bonus/commission is guaranteed and an average income can be taken. If you are applying for a joint income then multiply your two salaries by 2.25.

| Example: | Salary 1 | = | £30,000 |
|----------|----------|---|---------|
|          | Salary 2 | = | £15,000 |
|          |          |   |         |
|          | Total    |   | £45,000 x 2.25 |
|          |          |   |         |
|          |          | = | **£101,250** |

This figure (£101,250) is the **maximum** which the lender will advance unless there are special circumstances. The lender will need proof of your income, probably your last three pay slips. If you are self-employed, then you will need to produce the last three years certified accounts.

If you are considering an older property then the lender is unlikely to offer as much of the purchase price because of the obvious risks. Perhaps only 70% will be available so you should only consider such a move if you have adequate savings. Brand new homes however are less of a risk as they are (probably) less prone to structural defects and come with the NHBC (see later) guarantee for 10 years.

## Who will lend the money?

The mortgage market has traditionally been a rich source of income for a variety of financial institutions. After all, the lender had good security for their loan during its life. Property was traditionally the best form of collateral - it is not as if the borrower could up-sticks with his home to another country. But during the recent economic recession, many lenders have retrenched and some have pulled out of the market altogether.

## Banks

Banks, somewhat surprisingly are rather late-comers to this type of business. However in 1993 they made 390,000 loans to private purchasers. The average advance was £47,400 (£52,300 to new purchasers and £46,900 to second-hand purchasers). This represents about one quarter of the market share. Banks have tended to attract their own traditional investor i.e. those who have been with the bank for many years.

## Building societies

Building societies have been in this game for many years and therefore bring a wealth of experience to the home-buyer. In 1993 the average advance they made was just over £46,000 (with the average dwelling price being £64,000). Building societies have tended to be more aggressive in their approach to attracting new business and often offer an entire home-mover's package including financial advice and assistance. But by the same token, they may be more conservative in the amount which they are prepared to lend you. Building societies are often allied to particular insurance companies. For example the Halifax and Sun Alliance. In return for offering a competitive rate, it may be a condition that the lender takes care of your insurance needs for you. Indeed the annual insurance premium may be added to your monthly repayment and collected directly from your account. This is not an unfair or restrictive term, but merely part of the deal on offer. If you are unhappy, then you have the choice to look elsewhere. In any event, once you have been paying your mortgage regularly for some time, the lender will usually permit you to go into the open market for insurance provided they are happy with the level of cover which you arrange.

## Insurance companies

Insurers have traditionally offered top-up loans to house buyers who fall short of their mortgage requirement. For example a bank may only be prepared to lend you 80% of the purchase price leaving you with a shortfall of maybe 10 or 15%. Some of the larger insurance companies are now also in the mortgage market proper and will operate under similar lending rules to those of a bank or building society. In general however, insurance companies tend to lend to lower risk applicants. If you are considering such a mortgage, you probably won't be able to approach the lender direct, but will have to enlist the support of a mortgage broker. The broker will not charge you a fee (unless this is part of his usual trading conditions and you are made fully aware), but makes his money by claiming commission from the lender.

## Brokers/intermediaries

Brokers, intermediaries, financial advisers etc., masquerade under a variety of names. The word cowboy may spring to mind in many cases particularly given the support of a recent Office of Fair Trading report which said that advisers were selling the most lucrative commission-driven home loans rather than offering the best [independent] advice. The report was particularly critical of the selling of endowment mortgages which can generate as much as £800 in commission per £50,000 of mortgage. Given that over 60% of new mortgages are endowment-linked there is clearly scope for a blurring of the decision-making process. Mortgages are currently not regulated by the Financial Services Act and there is no requirement on the industry to give the best [impartial] advice.

However, this is not to tar all advisers with the same brush and indeed there are many who can provide you with a speedy, efficient and cost-effective service. For first-time buyers particularly, the mortgage market may appear very muddled and confusing. This remember on top of an already potentially problematic and daunting experience involving solicitors, surveyors and estate agents. A broker who can shoulder at least some of this responsibility may be very attractive indeed. A broker may also be very handy if you are potentially an unusual borrower, for example if you are self-employed and do not have a regular income which can be declared. Also, unusual or expensive projects may be beyond your expertise or funds. A broker however may use his extensive contacts and experience to look at the market as a whole and seek a workable solution to your initial problem. This may entail an approach to two or more lenders and the detailing of several agreements to satisfy your need.

There are clearly pitfalls when transacting business through brokers or other intermediaries, particularly given the scant legislative protection. The Personal Investment Authority (PIA) which replaced the likes of FIMBRA, Lautro and IMRO has at the moment no regulatory role over such mortgage business, so you should choose your adviser very carefully, ideally on a personal recommendation. It is very easy to be taken in by a silken-tongued salesman/adviser. This is true in all aspects of life, but particularly so in the field of financial products because we are often buying a dream and are totally ignorant of the market. Always consider all of the small print and if in doubt either walk away from the proposal or speak with your solicitor who should be able to clarify exactly what you are letting yourself in for. Only insurance brokers registered with the Insurance Brokers Registration Council can actually call themselves brokers. Their trade body is the British Insurance and Investment Brokers Association. Give them a ring to ensure that your adviser is a member (see Useful Addresses).

**Centralised lenders**
These are new and dynamic lenders forged out of the mortgage deregulation of the 1980's. The term "centralised" comes from the fact that they operate from a single, central office and have no branches. In their early days they

offered some fairly revolutionary products such as 100 per cent, fixed-rate and capped mortgages. Of course all of the big lenders have had to follow suit to grab an ever decreasing share of the market and as a result some of the centralised lenders have fallen on hard times. Now they tend to offer specialist mortgages for smaller, niche groups of customers, often those rejected by the banks and building societies. The Mortgage Business for example has developed two products to help customers avoid paying the full cost of mortgage indemnity guarantees (the insurance policy which indemnifies the lender in the event of a shortfall between the amount of the money borrowed and the resale value of the property - many of the large insurers have been crippled by such losses in the wake of the tidal wave of repossessions).

Centralised lenders obtain their lending money in a different way from the mainstream lenders. They get their money from the international money markets. Interest rates here tend to be lower so that the centralised lenders can borrow more cheaply. Couple this with the lack of a costly branch network, and mortgages can often be made available more cheaply to customers. However, centralised lenders came in for some severe criticism in the early 1990's for failing to drop their interest rates. This was largely because they did not have the cushion of investors such as the banks to let them drop their rates quickly enough. This problem has now been largely eradicated.

**What type of mortgage?**
There is much technically confusing jargon associated with the mortgage market. This may have contributed to many house buyers taking out an unsuitable loan. Ignorance has traditionally been the greatest key to financial reward for those in the financial services industry. So it's **very** important to make an informed decision on the best product for your particular circumstances having weighed up **all** the facts and read the small print.

*Repayment mortgage*
This is the traditional type of loan although much less popular today. It may also be termed a "Capital and Interest" mortgage. Your monthly repayment is made up of part repayment of the original sum you borrowed (capital) and part interest on that loan. It is the easiest type of mortgage to understand because your repayment term (typically twenty-five years), incorporates how much you have borrowed and the prevailing interest rate. At the start of the repayment period you will be paying mostly interest. But soon you will start to chip away at the capital sum itself. Ten years into a twenty-five year term, your annual mortgage statement will be easy to understand as it will show how much you have to repay.

Many building societies keep monthly repayments the same over the repayment period. This is called the Constant Net System but will only prevail if interest rates stay the same. Most of the banks tend to use the Gross Profile System which means that payments during the early years are lower. But as with all repayment mortgages, the proportion of each payment representing the capital repayment gradually increases. The net payment after tax relief (MIRAS) slowly increases also under the gross profile system. The gross profile system can be very attractive to first-time buyers who may be particularly strapped for cash during the early years of their mortgage. With all types of repayment mortgage there is usually no built-in insurance cover. The mortgagee will therefore probably stipulate life assurance as being an additional requirement before the loan is advanced. This insurance will repay the mortgage in the event of the borrower's death.

*Endowment mortgages*
Endowment mortgages have become increasingly common and popular. They have also regrettably come in for some serious criticism and scrutiny from the regulatory authorities. Under such a policy you only pay off the interest on the capital with your monthly repayment. You will not start to chip away at the capital. In addition to the interest payment you will also be required to invest in a life insurance policy which should at its time of maturity, have grown sufficiently to pay off the capital sum. Like the repayment mortgage and life assurance combination, so a life policy would cover the debt in the event of the borrower's death. You will therefore make two payments every month, one to the bank or building society and one to the insurance company which has issued the life policy. There are basically two types of endowment mortgage:

• with-profits
This is the most common and keeps the costs down by being linked to an inexpensive life policy. In most cases it should repay the capital sum on maturity and may also provide a healthy windfall by way of a surplus. Also, every two or three years, the insurance company adds a bonus to the value of your with-profits policy, according to how well their investments are performing. These bonuses are guaranteed and cannot be taken away.

• unit-linked
Under such a scheme the monthly payments are invested in managed funds. These policies have become popular because they offer the chance of an increased return if the investments are sound. But they can be risky too as, *"investments may go down as well as up ..."*

With both of these types of endowment policy, it is worth bearing in mind that the insurance company offering the life cover may insist on a medical if you are over a certain age, or suffer from certain medical complaints. High-risk adventurers should also not be surprised if obtaining cover proves to be difficult!

Endowment policies should not be viewed as an investment tool for reaping rich, short-term gains. There has been much publicity surrounding them and the fact that countless home owners could be at risk if their life policies fail to perform sufficiently well to pay off the capital sum. Now it is clear that if you cash in your endowment policy within the first five years, expect to lose around £1,800 in real terms. If you surrender your policy after five years but before maturity, you may do better than a repayment mortgage, but only if investment returns have been strong relative to mortgage interest rates. If you hold on to the endowment for the *full* term then you stand a reasonable chance of doing better than those with repayment mortgages. In general it is likely that most borrowers will be saddled with policies which levy higher than average charges that further erode their poor investment performance. Many needy people may well have to borrow to keep the policy running. The Director General of the Office of Fair Trading (OFT, see Useful Addresses) recommends that less well-off people who cannot count on always being able to pay the monthly premiums should buy repayment mortgages. Remember that once you have been sold an endowment you are effectively locked into it unless you want to lose money by cashing it in. Even if you pay all your premiums throughout the life of the policy, there is no **guarantee** that you won't be out of pocket. Also if MIRAS tax relief is abolished outright, on a £50,000 mortgage, an endowment will work out £300 to £500 more expensive in real terms.

You should not surrender an endowment policy unless your circumstances are extreme. If you really have no option, then you should compare what your insurance company will offer as a surrender value with the policy's sale value on the second-hand market. A number of companies specialise in the used market and may well pay more for your policy.

### Pension related mortgages

A pension mortgage can prove to be a convenient and tax-effective means to buy your house. By paying a proportion of your income into a pension scheme, a fund is established which should provide a retirement income. In essence, you pay interest over the term of the mortgage (like an endowment policy). On retirement, the money which you have been investing in the pension scheme can be used for two purposes: firstly to provide you with a retirement income and secondly as a tax-free cash lump sum to pay off the capital element of the mortgage. Currently pension contributions qualify for tax relief at the highest rate of income payable. There are various rules which govern the type of pension mortgage which you may be eligible for, so again be prepared to consider all the options carefully. It is worth bearing in mind however that although they are tax efficient you would be repaying the loan out of your pension benefits. You should therefore consider making alternative arrangements as you get older so that your pension benefits remain untouched. Also a pension plan does not provide life cover in the event of early death.

## 2.3 THE SURVEY

A critical part of any property transaction, the survey is important for two main reasons:

1. If there is a mortgage involved, to show that there is sufficient security in the property.
2. To check upon the structure, internal and external condition of the building and to make recommendations in respect of remedial works where necessary.

There are three principal types of report which serve different purposes. They differ in how much they cost and in how much protection they afford the purchaser where errors have been made.

### (i) A valuation report

This is a very basic assessment of the property's worth and should be carried out by a qualified surveyor. The report is really only for the benefit of the lender and will cost between £150 and £200. It is little more than a cursory visual inspection checking that the property has four walls, a roof and all the other bits which a house or flat should have. Most valuation reports are carried out under Royal Institution of Chartered Surveyors (RICS) (see Useful Addresses) or Incorporated Society of Valuers and Auctioneers (ISVA) guidelines. The brief of the surveyor is to assess how much the property would sell for on the open market at the date of inspection. In reaching the valuation he will consider:

- the age and type of property.
- its construction and general state of repair.
- local amenities.
- easements and rights of way which may bind the buyer.
- the local housing market.

If you buy your home relying purely on the information in the valuation report, you may be taking something of a risk, particularly with older properties. The report is principally for the benefit of the lender and gives no guarantees in respect of the structural soundness of the property. A valuation report is not therefore to be seen as a policy of insurance. It may be that some time after you move in, quite major defects become apparent. The surveyor was clearly under an obligation to act professionally and owes his clients a duty of care. However, unless the defect was physically obvious and a failure to pick up on a problem amounted to negligence, it is unlikely that you could pursue a claim for compensation.

### (ii) A home buyer's report
These are a relatively new type of report and bridge the gap between the scant valuation report and full-blown (and expensive) structural survey. Such a report is commissioned by the purchaser and not the lender. The report gives more information and is produced on standard RICS and ISVA forms. Indeed the report is concluded following several pages of standard questions relating to the exterior and interior of the building. However it does not include details of every minor defect. The potentially major problems such as damp and subsidence should be picked up but the report only covers those parts which are reasonably accessible. So roof spaces are only inspected if to do so would not involve Olympian athleticism. Main walls are examined from ground level whilst some damp meter readings may be taken.

### (iii) A full structural survey
This is a form of insurance as it is the most detailed and expensive type of report. A proper survey should cover all aspects of the property, from the type of soil and vegetation in the garden, right up to the pointing on the chimney stack. It will also state whether any repairs are required and the probable costs associated. It is most often bought by potential purchasers of either expensive or possibly troublesome properties. Although costly, the survey may be a very valuable tool in seeking a reduction of the purchase price. The vendor may have accepted your original offer subject to a satisfactory survey. If the survey comes back with a long list of problems, some of which are serious, you will have ample ammunition to amend your offer downwards.

If the surveyor has failed to pick up on points which a reasonably competent member of his profession ought to have done, and you suffer loss as a result, you may well have a claim against him for compensation. In practice, of course, the surveyor would not be personally liable from his own pocket. All professionals carry indemnity insurance to cover negligence claims. The problem should first be directed to the surveyor concerned giving him the opportunity to comment and defend his corner. It is unlikely at the outset that your claim will be welcomed with open arms. The firm concerned may well refer you to their terms and conditions which purport to limit or exclude their liability. But such terms are subject to a test of reasonableness under the Unfair Contract Terms Act 1977. A full structural survey means just that and may run into thousands of pounds.

Given these factors, avoiding liability altogether may be rather difficult for the surveyors and their insurers. If your first approach fails you may need to enlist the support of another surveyor highlighting those aspects of the original survey which were lacking. Immediately this can start to become an expensive process particularly if you reach an impasse with the professionals concerned. You will probably have to see a solicitor experienced in negligence matters to stand any chance of success. You will also need to be perseverant and reasonable - difficult attributes to strive for following an already distressing and expensive transaction. One positive alternative is the arbitration scheme run by the Institute of Arbitrators under the auspices of the RICS. For a small fee you can get an independent decision which is binding on both parties. If you win you should get your fee back plus compensation. The downside is that if you lose, you will have lost the right to subsequently take the matter to court. The surveyor has to agree to arbitration. If he does not, then your claim must be referred to a court hearing.

If you are successful in your claim, the measure of damages (compensation) which you will be entitled to may come as something of a surprise to many. It is not the value of the remedial costs. It is however the difference in value of the property had you known of the problems prior to purchase. In some cases although the defects may be serious their effect on the purchase price may have been negligible. Suing in such instances may therefore prove to be a fruitless and expensive exercise. Be guided on the merits of litigation by a solicitor.

## 2.4 THE NHBC
The National House Building Council (see Useful Addresses) offers a type of warranty on new properties for ten years called "Buildmark". It is largely because of this that many purchasers will not pay for a survey but instead rely on the valuation report. In any event new developments are less likely, statistically to suffer major structural problems than their older counterparts. A summary of NHBC protection:

- in the first twelve months cover on mechanical parts such as plumbing and central heating.

- in the first twenty-four months the builder will be liable to put right any defects which result from a failure to comply with the minimum standards of workmanship.
- for the third to tenth year the property which is not covered by your own buildings policy, may be the subject of a Buildmark claim.

NHBC protection is clearly very valuable but remember that it is only valid for ten years from the date of first purchase and not the date on which you may have subsequently acquired the property.

## 2.5 FIXTURES AND FITTINGS

What you leave behind and what goes with you to your new home is not a matter for legislative control. It is purely a private arrangement between vendor and purchaser. Fixtures are generally fitted to the property or adjoining land. Curtain rails for example are usually fixtures but the curtains themselves are not. If you wish to leave the curtains then it is up to you whether you "throw them in" with the purchase price or agree a separate price with the purchaser. Remember that such agreements may be important to the buyer if he is looking to avoid paying Stamp Duty. As a guide the following can be considered:

### Fixtures
- Plumbing.
- Bathroom suites.
- Wiring.
- Fitted fires.
- Built-in furniture.
- Floor tiles.
- Light switches.
- Door fittings.
- Fixed garden sheds/greenhouses.
- Permanent shelving.
- Curtain fixtures.
- Kitchen units.

### Fittings
- Refrigerator.
- Freezer.
- Dishwasher.
- Tumble drier.

- Microwave.
- Curtains.
- Carpets.
- Detachable floor coverings.
- Removable shelves.
- Light shades and bulbs.
- Garden furniture.

The vendor will be sent a detailed questionnaire before exchange of contracts. This opportunity should be used wisely to avoid any subsequent disputes over fixtures or fittings which you thought were being left behind.

## 2.6 TAX
There is an old saying - there are two certainties in life - death and tax. Property transactions can feel like death to many people particularly on the date of completion and as always central government will intervene where there is the opportunity to raise revenues by taxing movers! Stamp Duty has already been considered as one type of tax. There are others:

### Income tax
If the proposed property is to be your principal residence then you can apply for tax relief on the first £30,000 of your mortgage. This is called Mortgage Interest Relief at Source (MIRAS). This means that you will pay 85p of each £1 of interest on the first £30,000 of your loan. Only one £30,000 exemption is allowed per property - not per purchaser. On buying your home or taking out a mortgage your solicitor will ask you to sign the MIRAS forms so that in future everything should be taken care of. Thereafter your monthly repayment is calculated net of basic rate tax relief. If your lender is not covered by the MIRAS scheme of if you are self-employed you will have to pay mortgage interest gross and then claim the relief from the Inland Revenue. Government policy on mortgages and income tax relief has been somewhat haphazard. It now seems that the current government is intent on gradually abolishing MIRAS altogether.

### Inheritance tax
Formerly called death duties, inheritance tax or IHT kicks in if you die leaving assets valued at more than £154,000. The rate of tax on this sum is currently 40%. But there are exemptions, the most notable of which is that if on death your assets are left to your spouse, then no IHT is payable (but it may be if left to your children). But this spouse exemption does not apply to unmarried co-habitees. If IHT is due, then the surviving partner is in no better

position than anyone else. Lifetime tax planning is therefore important to ensure that your loved ones are not saddled with massive tax bills following your death. Remember that the value of your estate is assessed by considering the total value of *everything* you own, not just your property.

## Capital gains tax (CGT)
This is basically what it seems, a tax charged on a capital gain. Fortunately there are exemptions to protect you when buying and selling property. If this were not the case, tax may be payable on the difference in value between the original purchase and current selling price. If the property which you buy and sell is your main residence then no CGT is payable. Everybody, whether married or not has an annual exemption allowance to set off against CGT. Currently this figure is £6,000. But there are two important differences between married and unmarried couples:

1. A gift from one spouse to another does not attract CGT. Gifts between cohabitees may.

2. A married couple only has one main residence exemption from CGT between them. Unmarried couples however each have their own main residence exemption if they own and occupy separate homes.

CGT may also be payable if you let your home or part of your home to a private tenant. (See Chapter 6 for further detail.) If in any doubt always speak with a tax adviser or the Revenue itself.

## 2.7 ESTATE AGENTS
Popular people estate agents. Regrettably this is not the case at all. They have a reputation as having the smoothest of silken tongues, the toughest of hard skin and the deepest of deep pockets. In the popularity stakes they probably rank alongside the tax man and used car dealers. Some of this criticism may be justified. Indeed during the property boom of the 1980's many agents did make a lot of money using their finely tuned and imaginative skills. A broom cupboard could be sold as an aircraft hangar with an appropriate asking price. The late 1980's also saw the proliferation of national chains of estate agents often backed by the major building societies and banks. Being economic with the truth or by employing other sharp practices such as putting in false offers still prevail to a certain extent today. But in fairness to the profession it would be wrong to tag its members as being any worse than any of the other service professionals. In any event, the property slump and tighter judicial control have meant that consumers are now generally better served and better protected. Obviously the watchword is still very much caution - but this

should go without saying when buying such an expensive commodity. Estate agents are governed by the laws of contract and agency, the Estate Agents Act 1979 and the Property Misdescriptions Act 1991.

If you are selling your property be prepared to negotiate the commission rate payable. It will vary according to the type of agreement you enter into but generally should not exceed 3.5%. Check that there are no fees payable up front and that commission is only due on a completed sale. Are there any hidden extras in respect of photos, advertising or For Sale boards? In effect you can enter into one of four types of sale agreement.

### (i) Sole agency
This means that you are tied to one agent, only for a set period, perhaps twelve weeks initially. The commission rate should be the lowest as only one agent stands to benefit from your sale. During such an agreement you are still at liberty to try and sell privately.

### (ii) Multiple agency
Here your particulars are placed with several agents with the hope that more potential buyers will see them. The agent selling receives the commission (which is higher than for sole agency agreements).

### (iii) Joint sole agents
Here two or more agents act together and will share the commission if *either* makes the sale.

### (iv) Sole selling rights
This is to be avoided if possible. Simply, you agree to let one agent sell your property and agree a commission payable to him. But the commission will be payable however the property is sold - even if you do so privately.

### The Property Misdescriptions Act 1991
This is a welcome piece of legislation introduced with the aim of controlling estate agents' imaginative pens. Estate agentese is well-known, *"deceptively large .... stunning views .... tranquil setting ....."* could actually be *"box room.... overlooking a coal mine .... adjacent to the M25....."* The test under this Act is whether the particulars of the property (verbal or written) would mislead a reasonable person. Of course there is room for subjectivity - one agent's opinion on decor may not be the same as yours. But misleading information such as, *"tranquil setting"* above could well give rise to an offence. If in any doubt speak with your local Trading Standards Department. It is their offices who bring prosecutions under the Act.

## Estate Agents Act 1979

Under this Act, agents owe their clients a legal duty to find the best available sale. It is also "undesirable practice" if they fail to pass on all offers to you or otherwise discriminate between potential buyers. Again such practices should be reported to the Trading Standards Department. For example if the agent considers the offer too low and fails to pass the information on (not their decision to take!) a breach of the Act may have occurred.

## National Association of Estate Agents (NAEA)

This Association was established in 1962 with the aims of (amongst others), safeguarding the public against restrictive practices, protecting the general public against fraud, misrepresentation and malpractice. Therefore always look for an agent who is a member as it should show that higher standards have to be attained and that the member is bound by the Association's Rules of Conduct. If you have a complaint against a member then it should be made in writing and sent to the Association's Executive Committee (see Useful Addresses). If the complaint is upheld the member may be punished by one or more of the following: caution, reprimand, fine, reclassification of membership, suspension or ultimately expulsion.

## Ombudsman For Corporate Estate Agents (OCEA)

The OCEA was established in 1990 to provide an independent service for dealing with disputes between Member Agencies and consumers who are either buyers or sellers of residential property in the UK. The scheme covers the majority of major corporate residential estate agency chains in the UK (such as those run by building societies). The Ombudsman will consider complaints of unfair treatment, maladministration and infringement of legal rights. He cannot deal with complaints if they are not against a Member Agency, are being dealt with by a court, relate to a survey dispute, are for more than £100,000, the complaint is more than 12 months old or if it is sent to the Ombudsman more than 6 months after you receive a settlement offer from the Member Agency concerned. To complain you must first utilise the Member Agency's internal procedure. If this proves fruitless, formulate your complaint in writing to the Ombudsman (see Useful Addresses). The Ombudsman will then investigate your complaint and ultimately send his decision to both parties. You are not bound to accept his decision but the Member Agency will be bound to pay compensation of up to £100,000 provided you accept the payment on a full and final settlement basis. Otherwise you are free to seek legal redress elsewhere.

## 2.8 A PRIVATE SALE

Most people do tend to use estate agents to sell their property. However there is clearly room for conflict if you manage to find a purchaser without any assistance. In most cases the agent will claim that they were responsible for introducing the prospect and as such entitled to their commission. This can be quite a difficult assertion to defend as even if the agent had seemingly done little to sell your property, a "For Sale" sign could be taken as evidence of the introduction. True enough if you struck the deal with an unsuspecting purchaser whilst at the supermarket or down at the local, then technically the agent has had no involvement and should not be entitled to commission. But proving this is another matter altogether and tenacious estate agents may go as far as sending a threatening solicitor's letter. Because of this potential problem it is important that you clarify the extent of the agent's contractual obligation at the outset. If the contract is strictly no sale, no fee then you should not have to pay anything (subject to you staying with the agent for the agreed minimum period). Other contracts may compel you to pay a fee if a purchaser is introduced who is ready, willing and able to complete the transaction. Under such an agreement you could still have to pay a fee if you took the property off the market or if you found a "private" purchaser.

## 2.9 GAZUMPING/GAZUNDERING

Horror stories abound at this practice and its legality. In Scotland where there is an altogether different system for household purchase and sale, the problem does not exist. Because you are not legally locked into a purchase/sale until contracts have been exchanged, a vendor is at liberty to accept a higher offer right up to the point of exchange. This is called gazumping and is particularly prevalent in a seller's market. In a buyer's market, the situation is rather different in that the purchaser may put in a lower offer (gazundering) right at the last minute, effectively forcing the hand of the vendor. At present there is no legal redress for such practices. It is just a very painful part of an already hazardous property exchange process.

## 2.10 SCOTLAND

The Scottish system is much praised by the sasenachs as being less complicated and more user-friendly. In essence the offer is binding at the outset, so should only be made once a mortgage has been agreed. Once the property has been surveyed and an offer made, both party's solicitors exchange contracts by an exchange of letters or "missives". The advantages are clear - once your offer is accepted, the deal must go ahead. There is no room for gazumping. The principal disadvantage is the upfront cost. Surveys have to be paid for **before** offer. If the survey indicates potential problems with the property, you would effectively pull out of the deal before making the offer. If this happens on several potential purchases, the exercise can get rather expensive!

## 2.11 AUCTIONS

Auctions are a relatively new, but increasingly popular way to buy property. But be aware of the legal considerations. Much like a motor auction, once the hammer comes down on the deal, the house is yours. You cannot back out. If you buy a real lemon of a car, you might be in a position to write off a few hundred or even thousand pounds. But could you do the same in respect of a £100,000 home? Buying at auction can be a bargain. The reason for this is simple. The owners of the properties in the sale, whether repossessed or otherwise, are out for a quick deal. An auction catalogue is usually released two to four weeks before the actual date. During this period there is much to be done to protect your legal position. In particular you must complete a survey, have satisfactory searches and have a mortgage offer in place. This latter point is critical because if your bid is accepted, you will have to pay 10% of the purchase price immediately, with the balance within 28 days. If subsequent to the hammer coming down, you change your mind or otherwise fail to complete the transaction, you will be in breach of contract. At the least, you will forfeit the 10% deposit. A solicitor must be instructed prior to the auction to ensure that you will acquire a good title and that there are no sitting tenants etc.

## 2.12 REMOVAL FIRMS

Another somewhat emotive issue, so it is important that you shop around to find a firm that you are happy with and offers adequate insurance. Again personal recommendations are probably the best. The firm will ask you to sign a contract. This will almost certainly contain terms and conditions seeking to either limit or exclude their liability in the event of breakages etc. Check the small print carefully. The terms must be fair and reasonable and will be subject to the Unfair Contract Terms Act 1977. In terms of the work of the removal firm itself, it must be to a reasonable standard under the Supply of Goods and Services Act 1982. So removers owe you a contractual duty, but also a duty of care in negligence. You can claim under either or both for losses and damage resulting from a lack of care. This will include the cost of repair, the cost of replacing lost items and reasonable redecorating costs if applicable.

The company concerned will almost certainly offer some form of insurance. This is probably a good buy provided you have read and understood all the policy stipulations (for example cover may be voided if you have interfered with the packing rather than leaving it to the "experts"). If insurance is offered, single liability for damage will be limited to a low figure. If you do not accept this you will have to fight out your case in court. Always look for firms which are members of the British Association of Removers (see Useful Addresses). If both parties agree, it can appoint an independent arbitrator to consider the complaint and give a decision which is binding.

## 2.13 SOLICITORS

Assuming that your DIY skills do not extend to buying and selling property, you will have to instruct a solicitor to do the job for you. Estate agents we have already seen have a poor reputation. So too solicitors. For years solicitors made lots of money from conveyancing and probate work. Today, due to the loss of their monopoly and a generally more cost-conscious public, fees have been slashed. Indeed the market is now so cut-throat that solicitors may be forced to cut corners to protect their margins. Again you should be prepared to phone around to get a feel for the firm and an estimate of their likely costs. Remember that if you are buying and selling, the fee will be commensurately higher. The figure you are quoted, typically £250 - £350 for a purchase, will be exclusive of VAT and other disbursements (Land Registry fees, local search fees, Stamp Duty, mortgage indemnity premium etc.). So a bargain quote of £200 will not be all that it seems.

Licensed conveyancers rose form the ashes of the conveyancing monopoly in the 1980's. Members of the National Association of Conveyancers (see Useful Addresses) can do pretty much the same work as solicitors in private practice. However they must have five years experience and carry sufficient indemnity insurance. Surprisingly there are relatively few licensed conveyancers practising today and the market for conveyancing professionals generally, did not expand as anticipated. Licensed conveyancers may be slightly cheaper and may offer a more streamlined service. But these short-term benefits must be viewed against potential problems. Particularly complex issues such as to title or sitting tenants may in the long-term, have to be referred on to a solicitor anyway.

Complaints against solicitors are commonplace, particularly in regard to property transactions. Indeed many sole practitioners give the rest of the profession something of a bad name by taking on more work than they can reasonably cope with and then either "losing" clients money or failing to complete formalities on time. Complaints generally fall into three categories - overcharging, poor work and negligence. In respect of overcharging, solicitors cannot provide a detailed estimate as a guarantee of the final bill. But just as if you take your car into a garage and put a financial limit on the work to be carried out, so a solicitor ought to keep you informed as and when these limits are reached. A commonsense approach should be adopted and in any event the bill must be fair and reasonable. If not, then the nature of the complaint will depend upon the type of work which the solicitor did. If it was a litigious matter in which court proceedings had been commenced then the solicitor is required to provide a detailed breakdown of the work done. If this fails to resolve the dispute, the matter is referred to a process called taxation. But if, as is the case with conveyancing, the work is non-contentious you can ask for a Certificate of Remuneration within twenty-eight days of the date of the bill. Under this procedure it is the Law Society which considers the paperwork and decides whether the bill is fair and reasonable or what other sum would be so in all the circumstances. Unlike taxation this service is free and often highly effective.

If the complaint is about poor or slow or unprofessional work, then in the first instance it should be referred to the solicitor's internal complaints handling procedure (if he's part of a firm). Usually the case is given to the senior partner. But of course this process can never be truly impartial and if a solution is not reached, a brief account of the problem should be referred to the Solicitors' Complaints Bureau (SCB, see Useful Addresses). If the nature of the complaint is that the solicitor has caused you distress but did not incur any financial loss, then the SCB provides a system aimed at quickly resolving such problems informally. It can award up to £1000 in compensation.

The SCB will also consider much more serious complaints of negligence, which in property cases, could amount to losses of tens of thousands of pounds.

# Chapter 3

## Insurance

Now that you have bought your dream home or indeed are renting it, you will want to protect both the structure and fabric of the building together with all your personal contents. Insurance generally is something of an emotive issue - for years we may pay our annual buildings premiums without a claim or default on payment and then suddenly when a claim for subsidence arises, the insurer either does not want to know or says that you are woefully under insured. There is also ample scope for disputes and complaints about policy wording and interpretation in the field of contents insurance. Does my policy cover accidental damage in respect of personal effects, and if so how are personal effects legally defined? Of course this chapter is not intended to give financial advice or to discuss the range of individual policies available from each of the insurers. However it is intended to unravel some of the mysterious terminology and types of cover which are most suitable and to consider possible legal remedies if it all goes horribly wrong. For the homeowner only two types of insurance will be considered here - building and contents. Both types are essential although regrettably, perhaps as many as 25% of households do not insure their contents. Whilst this is understandable - after moving there may be many more pressing demands on an already stretched budget or the perception of insurance offering little by way of tangible benefit may prove just too much, non-insurance could prove to be disastrous. In 1994 there were 1.3 million burglaries reported whilst many more suffered from fires and flooding. During the winter, parts of the west of Scotland were hit by exceptionally heavy rains. Many families who had not insured were left with no home, no possessions and no compensation.

One of the covenants of your mortgage will compel you to take out buildings insurance (buildings defines the fixed structure of a house - walls, floors, roof, plumbing, wiring and anything added to the property which is not readily removable such as bathrooms and fitted kitchens). After all your property is the only security for the mortgagee's loan so any damage to your home affects this security. Contents are loosely defined as anything which you would take with you on moving home, including the carpets. Outbuildings, walls, greenhouses and swimming pools would all be classified as buildings.

## 3.1 BUILDINGS INSURANCE
When you take out cover it is your responsibility to ensure that you have adequate cover. Bleating to the insurer after the event will not find favour. The policy itself will be designed to insure full rebuilding costs rather than its open market value. If the property is not adequately insured then the value of your claim will be averaged. This means that the amount claimed will be reduced proportionately according to the amount by which your home is under insured.

When you first buy your home, the surveyor/valuer will give his professional opinion on the rebuilding costs. The policy should be index-linked to the Housing Cost Index from the Royal Institution of Chartered Surveyors (RICS, see Useful Addresses). But this may not be enough to always protect your position. If there have been any improvements such as double glazing or a new conservatory, you must notify your insurers. Always keep copies of such correspondence. Remember that the duty to insure the buildings arises from the date of exchange of contracts. Your solicitor should arrange various options but it is worth shopping around. But surprisingly few people do. According to Association of British Insurers (ABI, see Useful Addresses) research, only 25% of homeowners consider the property market. If they did, savings of up to 50% could be achieved.

## Types of policy

In essence there are two types of policy - standard and wider cover. Standard policies normally list all the causes of damage that are covered. Though not exhaustive, the following should be included:

* fire, lightning, explosion, earthquake.
* storm, flood.
* subsidence (but subject to local restrictions).
* impact from accidents with cars, animals, aircraft and things falling from them - including frozen waste from airliners.
* impact from falling trees and branches.
* impact from TV aerials.
* water or heating oil leakages.
* theft or attempted theft, damage done by thieves and vandalism.
* riots, strikes and political disturbances.

But on the downside, most standard policies exclude the following:

* major frost damage.
* damage resulting from a lack of or poor maintenance to your property.
* electrical breakdown.
* storm and flood damage to gates and fences.
* damage resulting from war, sonic booms and nuclear contamination!

Wider cover, although more expensive, provides greater peace of mind by covering accidental damage. If you are an accident prone DIYer or if your property needs a lot of work, this type of cover can be a good investment.

**Types of cover**
There are generally two types; new for old or indemnity. Most new policies are of the new for old type which means that if your fitted bathroom is damaged by a flood, the insurance company will (subject to policy restrictions and conditions) replace it with a new one. Under an indemnity policy, the insurance company will take account of the age and condition of the damaged structure or items and not replace with new. Of course new for old policies are more expensive, but naturally offer peace of mind. All policies will have an excess - an amount of the claim which you have to pay. The cheaper your policy, generally the higher the excess will be. In high risk subsidence areas, the excess may run into several hundreds of pounds.

### 3.2 CONTENTS INSURANCE
Contents insurance is expensive and seemingly on an upwards spiral. Not surprising then that perhaps a quarter of all households still have no contents cover, or if they do are woefully under insured. But premiums could be reduced for the following reasons:
- security discounts.
- age-discounts for the over 50's.
- no-claims bonuses.
- neighbourhood watch schemes.
- increased excess.

Like buildings insurance, there are again two types, standard cover and standard plus accidental damage. Standard cover should extend to claims arising from:
- fire, flood, lightning, earthquake, explosion, fallen trees, water and oil leakages, car, trains or aircraft crashes, theft, riot, vandalism, subsidence.

It should also cover against costs incurred relocating to new accommodation if your home is made uninhabitable by one of the above. Personal liability cover is also usually included. Exclusions are:
- problems caused by fungus, vermin, insects or rot.
- problems caused by a lack of maintenance.
- problems that arise during prolonged absences from the property.
- damage caused by war and sonic booms!
- animals and plants.
- mechanical/electrical breakdown.
- theft of money unless forcible entry can be shown.

Contents premiums do vary widely but tend to depend on where you live and your claims history. There is also Insurance Premium Tax (IPT) to consider which is passed on directly to the consumer in the form of higher premiums. The insurance is usually calculated according to postcode. Some insurers have as many as eight rate bands and can vary from 18p per £100 insured in Scotland, to 40p per £100 in parts of London. Standard cover plus accidental damage can be a good buy, particularly if you are quite clumsy or you have lots of young children running around. But do check exclusions. An all-risks policy may also be worth considering. Naturally more expensive, such policies cover your insured belongings such as cameras etc., whilst away from the property itself.

Contents insurance can be bought on either a sum - insured or bedroom-rated basis. Under the former, you have to work out the replacement value of all your possessions and present this figure to the insurers. You effectively buy cover according to the value of your belongings. On a bedroom-rated policy you are insured for a fixed amount according to the number of bedrooms you have. Such policies have fixed levels of cover according to the size and location of your property. Bedroom-rated policies are therefore only cheaper provided you fall into the correct value bracket for your home. For example the insurer may state that your size of home in your area requires £30,000 of cover when you may only have £18,000 worth of contents. Conversely if your small home is chock full of antiques and valuable paintings, the fixed sum may not be sufficient.

## 3.3 MISUNDERSTOOD INSURANCE PHRASES
### Utmost good faith
This is a legal requirement of all insurance contracts. It means that you must answer all questions posed by the insurance company truthfully. But more significantly, you also have to disclose any relevant information about the insured risk, even if specific questions have not been put to you. Relevant does not mean whether **you** consider it important, but whether the information could affect the decision to offer you cover. If you do not disclose such information, the insurance company is at liberty to void the policy, refund your premium and effectively leave you uninsured.

### Loss adjustors
These are independent insurance experts instructed by your insurers to consider the substance of your claim. For example if a tree fell on to your roof, they may be asked to consider whether the condition of the tree prior to it falling over contributed to the damage.

## Loss assessors

You would appoint a loss assessor in the most complicated claims to negotiate settlement. Their fee will be deducted from your payment on a percentage commission basis.

## Contra proferentem

In insurance terms this means that if there is some doubt about the definition or interpretation of a policy, it should be applied in the most favourable way to the complainant (usually the policyholder). An example may be as follows:

> Martin is an avid fan of 1950's music. He cannot do anything around the household without music blaring from his portable CD player. Regrettably his pet Iguana called Bill Haley one day mistakes the CD player for a mouse and inflicts mortal damage to it. Martin claims on his household contents policy which has accidental damage cover. The insurer repudiates the claim saying only personal effects are covered. Martin seeks advice on the policy wording upon which the insurers have sought to rely. Because there is clearly some doubt about its interpretation, he successfully pleads the contra proferentem rule (i.e. most favourably to him) and is paid out for the partly digested CD player.

## Mitigation of loss

This is an important aspect of any civil claim and basically means that the claimant or plaintiff is under duty to minimise his loss. It is a fairly complicated legal phrase, but has two principal elements.

- the claimant must take all reasonable steps to avoid unnecessary losses. You cannot recover avoidable loss.
- where the claimant does take reasonable steps to mitigate the loss to him as a result of the other party's wrong, he can recover for losses incurred in so doing. In simple terms you could recover for loss incurred in reasonable attempts to avoid loss!

## To act as if uninsured

This is another popular term much used by insurance companies and in a sense is closely allied to mitigation of loss. It basically means that to protect your position and that of the insurance company, you must act as if you did not have an insurance policy, i.e. would your losses have been as great if you were uninsured or did you somehow fail to act as reasonably and as quickly as you ought to have done, simply because you knew that somebody else would be paying the bills? Here is an example:

> **Murray and Eileen live in a big, run-down home in the Outer Hebrides. They have a valid buildings insurance policy. At the bottom of the garden is a shed which houses their oil tank. The roof was half blown off during the early part of the winter, leaving the tank exposed to the elements. They knew there was a risk, but decided not to claim to the insurers until the spring when the winds had subsided. Later on that winter during a violent storm, the rest of the roof was blown off and a roof joist fell and ruptured the oil tank. A fire followed which gutted their Land Rover parked nearby. The insurance company only admitted part of their claim. Had Eileen and Murray been uninsured, they would have repaired the roof immediately thereby minimising the threat of further damage. Because they waited and failed to mitigate loss, the insurer concerned has taken a very hard line.**

## 3.4 FLAT INSURANCE AND SERVICE CHARGES

If you live in a block of flats, buildings insurance will usually be arranged on a group basis and the premium collected as part of the annual service charge. This will be done by the tenants association, management company or the freeholder himself. It is important that there is adequate cover - if the roof blows off in a storm one night, it will be all the residents' responsibility jointly to repair/replace. There is also scope for abuse by less than scrupulous managing companies or freeholders to arrange cover with the most "friendly" insurers. In respect of service charges generally, they have got to be incurred reasonably. The Landlord and Tenant Act 1985 may be of relevance:

- where a service charge is payable before costs of works etc. have been incurred, only a reasonable amount is payable. After the relevant costs have been incurred, adjustments may be made by repayment.
- service charges incurred more than eighteen months before a demand is made are not recoverable from tenants.
- tenants have the right to apply to the county court to challenge costs incurred by the landlord.
- a tenant has the right to request a summary of relevant costs incurred - the landlord must comply within one month of the request.
- a tenant who has obtained a summary of the relevant costs may require the landlord in writing within six months to provide reasonable facilities for:

- inspecting the accounts, receipts and other documents supporting the summary.
- copying this information.

• tenants have the right to request a summary of the buildings insurance - the landlord must supply this (a copy of the policy will do) within one month of the request.

• where there is a lease which requires the tenant to insure the buildings with an insurance company nominated by the landlord, the tenant is at liberty to challenge the company nominated. If you can therefore show that you can arrange comparable insurance elsewhere at a lower premium, then the landlord should sanction such a move.

In terms of contents insurance, this will usually be down to the flat-owner. Many mortgage lenders will arrange cover when you take out the loan. The premium will then be collected monthly as part of the annual repayment. It may be a condition of the mortgagee that you continue to take out their insurance. This is not an unfair contract term because you would have been at liberty to take out a loan elsewhere at the time. However, the lender may well be receptive to you arranging your contents insurance with another firm, provided you can produce written evidence to show that the cover is comparable and valid for the full twelve months.

### 3.5 CLAIMING, PROBLEMS AND EFFECTIVE COMPLAINING

Claiming under an insurance policy can be like a living hell. Claimants tend to fall into two categories - those who feel they must claim on an annual basis to get some value for money from the annual premium, and those who genuinely claim only when the need arises. In some cases this may be never even though thousands of pounds may have been committed to insurance premiums. Of course we have all heard of horrendous stories from friends and family who have had problems claiming. But then exceptional cases are always more newsworthy than those which proceed without a problem. Human nature. The insurance industry as a whole has a poor reputation when it comes to claims, but well supported, evidenced and reasonable submissions ought to pass through the insurers hands relatively speedily. Slow claims are just as often the fault of the claimant if you have only provided part of the information requested or generally been unhelpful. A failure to understand policy limitations can also be a major stumbling block.

Claiming is very much a question of commonsense and *generally* insurers will do what they can to assist. The market for household insurance is now very competitive so attaining the market edge in terms of customer service may be crucial to the insurance company concerned. Much business is now placed with the direct market - you simply pick up a telephone, give your details and cover is effected immediately. In such cases it is usual to pay by credit card or to agree to put a cheque in the post immediately. At this point, the contract of insurance is valid. Problems do occur with the automated quotation systems and it may be that your insurer subsequently says that it made a mistake and you owe some more. Provided you gave all the correct information and acted with utmost good faith at the time, the cost of the mistake should be borne by the insurance company. However, it may only offer a provisional quote on the telephone subject to a consideration of the proposal form. In such cases you may be asked to pay an additional sum. Many insurers offer twenty-four hour helplines giving easy access to a range of tradesmen and professionals. At a time of crisis, expert advice may be critical in ensuring that losses are mitigated and that the claims process gets off on the correct footing.

With all types of insurance claim, you must check to see whether your policy specifies a time limit for either notifying of a potential claim or submitting the correct claim form. If it is a burglary/theft/criminal damage claim, you will need a police report or crime reference number. If you require urgent building work, you may have to call out a twenty-four hour contractor to effect emergency repairs. Thereafter be guided by your insurers.

In terms of complaint there are several options open to you. Always act reasonably and try not to consider your grievance too subjectively. **Never** fight solely on a point of principle - you **will** fail. You should collate as much evidence in support as possible and, if necessary, be prepared to seek an independent expert's report, the cost of which may be added to your claim if successful. If you have arranged your business through a broker, he may be invaluable in assessing the merits of your complaint objectively. He will also have experience of insurance companies generally and should be able to direct you along the right path. If you have bought directly, then try to deal with the same individual every time you telephone or correspond. Always formulate and follow up your complaint in writing quoting the correct reference. Keep copies of all correspondence. Each insurance company will have its own complaints procedure which you should follow. If this fails, then effectively you have four options:

- sue for damages in the civil courts. Costly, complex, very lengthy and in all but the most serious cases, probably too risky.
- complain to the Insurance Ombudsman Bureau (IOB, see Useful Addresses).
- if not a member of the IOB scheme you could contact the Personal Insurance Arbitration Scheme (PIAS) which is operated by the

Association of British Insurers (see Useful Addresses). Here an independent arbitrator will be appointed to consider the complaint. It can be quite an effective remedy, but has two principal drawbacks: firstly both parties must consent to the procedure and secondly once you have agreed to arbitration, you lose your rights to sue in the civil courts.

* back down gracefully!

The Ombudsman is the most favoured scheme and deserves more attention. In essence the IOB was founded in 1981 by a group of major insurance companies to provide an independent and impartial method of resolving complaints. There are now over three hundred and fifty members of the IOB scheme. To be considered by the IOB your complaint must:

* have first been put to the insurance company concerned's own complaints procedure.
* be passed to the IOB within six months of the stalemate between you and the insurer.
* relate to a UK, Isle of Man or Channel Islands claim.
* relate to a claim on the administration or marketing of your policy.

It is also important to note that the IOB cannot intervene if the complaint is already being dealt with through the courts, or is in respect of a decision relating to cover. The IOB is a very busy office and in 1994 responded to 22,000 written enquiries and 30,000 telephone enquiries providing advice and assistance on the pursuit of complaints. If your complaint falls within the IOB's remit it will be handled by a consideration of all the papers and a liaison between the parties concerned. Experts may be consulted. Eventually (in 1994 the average case took 117 days to process) the Ombudsman will make a decision which will be sent in writing to you and the other party. The Ombudsman can award up to £100,000 in your favour, but his decision is not binding until accepted. If you reject the decision you are free to pursue other remedies. There is no cost to you and the insurance company is bound by the award. Also in 1994, the highest award was £167,600 and the lowest £3! The most common complaints to the IOB by far in terms of general insurance relate to motor and household disputes.

It is clear that if your insurer is a member of the IOB scheme, the procedure it offers for dealing with complaints can be of real value, particularly as you are not bound to accept any decision. The most recent review of the IOB has thrown up some topical problems of interest.

## Cancelling a policy mid-term

An insurance policy is like any other legally binding contract so unless the policy has been mis-sold by the insurer you cannot cancel it and expect a refund (in full or pro-rated). So once the policy has been properly issued there is no entitlement to recovery of any part of the annual premium, even if no claim has been made (but this strict legal interpretation is subject to individual insurance companies giving their policyholders the contractual right to cancel mid-term).

## Direct-debit problems

Many premiums are now collected over ten or twelve months by the convenient mechanism of direct debit. But this too is subject to breakdown so the Ombudsman has held that it is the responsibility of policyholders to ensure that the direct debit is functioning correctly, usually by reference to bank statements, before any claim can be laid at the insurer's door. But where the insurer has been at fault and failed to collect some payments, it may be expected to offer reinstatement of the policy (if lapsed) and waive some of the missing payments.

## Jewellery claims

Lost or stolen jewellery is often the subject of a complaint to the IOB in respect of the interpretation of a contents policy. The fact that such items often have an emotional as well as a high intrinsic value means that disputes are commonplace. Many policies allow the insurer to replace lost or stolen jewellery, but often you may want a cash settlement instead of a replacement and the insurer will offer a reduced amount because it could buy replacement jewellery at a discount. Many complaints are then made to the IOB claiming the difference between the replacement value and the discounted cash offer. Several issues are then considered to assess the legality of the insurer's actions, such as:

- *what is the appropriate discount?*
- *does the policy give the insurer the option between replacement and a cash settlement?*
- *is a replacement practicable?*

Also given that most policies now offer new for old cover, insurers will probably reserve their position - replacement is as new, but cash settlements would be on the basis of current value, reflecting a deduction in respect of the age, wear and tear etc.

## 3.6 LIABILITY INSURANCE

Fortunately we are not yet as litigation happy as our counterparts in the US. Seemingly any kind of accident is actionable and could give rise to multi-million dollar payments. But liability claims in the UK do arise with a surprising regularity. If a painter slips on an uneven paving stone and breaks his leg who is liable to compensate him? Most household policies offer substantial liability cover for such accidents but the question will be considered in more detail in Chapter 9.

# Chapter 4

## Building, improving, extending your property

In spite of some rather anomalous and bizarre structures and decor, fortunately there are building and planning controls in the UK. There has to be a framework within which all property and landowners operate which is consistent and readily understood. Regrettably, although the framework is clearly in existence, the mass of rules and regulations may be somewhat inconsistently applied. Many people will either buy land with the intention of building on it or may simply wish to modernise or improve their existing homes, perhaps by adding a conservatory. Knowing whether planning permission is required or whether building regulations must be complied with or even whether an architect is required is the aim of this chapter. It is clearly not exhaustive and because of the nature of this area of the law, takes on a rather general feel. If in any doubt always seek professional advice. A failure to do so could lead to catastrophic results. Not so long ago a man who failed to comply with enforcement procedures in respect of a property he had erected without planning permission, shot dead a local planning officer.

Everyday planning control is a matter for your local planning authority (LPA). Appeals against decisions of the LPA is to the Secretary of State for the Environment or to one of the members of the Planning Inspectorate appointed by him. This chapter deals primarily with the property owner. In respect of your neighbours, you can make representations to the LPA concerning any application for planning permission on adjoining land and appear at a local enquiry on appeal. Generally, the LPA does not owe a duty of care to you as a neighbouring landowner when granting permission, even if your interests may be adversely affected. Although of course the preparation process of local development plans does include extensive public consultation.

### 4.1 PLANNING PERMISSION

As a starting point permission is required for any development. Development is defined extremely broadly to encompass not only matters such as an extension but also plans which involve a change of use of the building concerned. The Town & Country Planning Act 1990 defines development further as, *"the carrying out of building, engineering, mining and other operations in, on, over or under land, or the making of any material change in the use of any buildings or other land..."*

Development specifically *excludes* internal or external improvements which do not materially affect the external appearance of the building. So an external redecoration job is not development and does not need permission. But converting a house into an office would be a change of use and require permission, even if no building work is required.

## Building from scratch

This is many people's dream. To simply buy a virgin piece of land miles from civilization and erect a home to suit your taste. You must of course obtain planning permission and the ease of doing so will depend upon several factors. Ordinarily you would be advised to apply for outline planning permission before you purchase the land. Outline permission simply means that the LPA agrees in principle to the building of some structure. It does not, at this stage, agree to any specific plans. But it is a step in the right direction and means that the land in question need not remain wholly undeveloped for ever. The procedure entails the submission of plans which simply show the size and proposed form of the development. If you have not yet bought the land, you would need to submit a Certificate B which confirms that the true owners are aware of the application. If approved, you would then need to get down to the nitty gritty application called an "application for approval of reserved matters." This is the process whereby the specific plans for your proposed development have to be considered and approved in the minutest detail.

Your application may well require the support of an architect. It is his job to draw up the plans, advise on local planning policy and to generally guide you through the entire process (which may take several months). The advantage of using a qualified architect who is a member of the Royal Institute of British Architects (RIBA, see Useful Addresses) is that he will carry indemnity insurance and be bound by RIBA's arbitration procedure in the event of a dispute. However such expertise does not come cheap and more minor drawings can be given to less qualified professionals. The architect will discuss the local situation with you and how your proposed development sits with the following:

### Access

This is one of the most important factors in the consideration of whether to grant planning permission. Safety will be an important facet of the access to your property, so consider approaching the Highways Authority.

### *Area of residential development?*

Every LPA has a master plan which details areas for continued residential development. If your plot of land does not fall within the master plan or is in say a green belt area, obtaining planning permission to build will be very difficult indeed. To avoid unnecessary heartache and expense, a simple telephone call to a local planning officer will tell you where your plans fit within the general scheme.

*Does your proposal involve the demolition of a listed building?*
If it does, then listed building consent is required in addition to full planning permission. Listed buildings are of course subject to special planning controls. There are currently three grades:

- grade i - exceptional interest (only 2% of listed buildings fall within this category.
- grade ii - particularly important buildings (4% of listed buildings).
- grade iii - the most common. These are buildings of special interest which should be preserved if at all possible. As there are only 6,000 Grade i listed buildings and around 20,000 Grade ii, the chance of obtaining consent to demolish them is remote.

*Is it in a conservation area?*
If it is then the planners will pay special attention to your application to ensure that it is entirely in keeping with the area. Obtaining permission to build in a conservation area may require some very well thought out and imaginative plans. To stay in keeping with the local character, particularly if your land is in a conservation area, may require rather more expensive building material than is usually the case.

**Where planning permission is not required**
The general rule is that any development requires planning permission. However parliament has fortunately agreed to permit certain types of development where formal permission is not required. The regulations for so doing are contained in the Town and Country Planning (General Development) Order 1988 - the GDO. This welcome piece of legislation sets out descriptions of permitted development (which are nonetheless subject to conditions). For our purposes, the following are most relevant:

**Part 1** - development within the curtilage of a dwelling-house.
**Part 2** - minor operations.
**Part 3** - changes of use, between classes of use.
**Part 4** - temporary buildings and uses.
**Part 9** - the carrying out of works required for the maintenance or improvement of an unadopted street or private way.

**Part 1 in further detail**
A dwelling-house is not accurately defined but it is clear that flats or blocks of flats are excluded from the definition. Consideration must also be given to whether the property in question is used exclusively for residential purposes.

The proposed development must be within the curtilage of the property. It has been defined as, *"the ground which is used for the comfortable enjoyment of a house or other building ... although it has not been marked off or enclosed in any way. It is enough that it serve the purpose of the house or building in some necessary or reasonably useful way."*

In terms of structural alterations or extensions etc., no planning permission is necessary under Part I of the GDO provided that the "new" building does not exceed the cubic content of the "original" building by 70 cubic metres or 15 per cent, whichever is the greater, subject to a maximum of 115 cubic metres. However in the case of terraced houses then the maximum increases are 50 cubic metres, 10 per cent and 115 cubic metres. This is fairly complex and you may need to avail yourself of professional help in assessing the proposed size of your development. It is worth noting also that "original" means in relation to buildings built before 1 July 1948 as existing at **that** date and, in relation to later buildings, as they were originally built and not as they may currently be with previous alterations. So in summary, no planning permission is required thus:

*Terraced houses*
New building is not increased by 50 cubic metres or 10 per cent.

*Other houses*
70 cubic metres or 15 per cent, whichever is the greater, subject to a maximum of 115 cubic metres.....**and**

- the proposed extension will not be higher than the original house (but if within two metres of the perimeter, then it must not exceed four metres in height).
- it will not project beyond the front line of the house where it abuts a public road or path.
- the area of ground covered by all buildings within the curtilage does not exceed fifty per cent of the total area of the curtilage excluding the ground area of the original house.
- it does not include the installation, alteration or replacement of a satellite dish.
- it does not consist of or include an alteration to any part of the roof.

In addition to simple extensions, the following can also be considered without the need for planning permission, but subject to conditions. Again if you are in any doubt, seek professional advice because the consequences of building without permission could be very painful indeed.

## Loft conversions

If the house is not to be enlarged, then any roof alternation is permitted, provided it does not materially alter the shape of the house. In other cases, development is limited to fifty cubic metres or forty cubic metres if a terraced house provided that this increase does not exceed the limit which apply to a house extension generally.

## Porches

But only if:

- the floor area does not exceed two square metres
- no part of it is more than three metres above ground level and
- no part of it is within two metres of a boundary to the road or footpath.

## Satellite dishes

OK provided:

- the dish does not exceed seventy centimetres in any dimension (or forty five cm if attached to a chimney)
- you only have one dish or other receiving equipment
- the highest part of the equipment is no higher than the highest part of your roof (or chimney if that is where it is attached).

## Swimming pools

OK provided this and other buildings within the curtilage is incidental to the enjoyment of the residence itself. So pools, summer houses, greenhouses, tool sheds will not require permission if all the following conditions are met:

- no part of it projects beyond the front line of the house where it faces a public highway
- its height does not exceed three metres or four metres if it has a ridged roof
- less than fifty per cent of the land will be covered by the new structure built since the erection of the house or since 1948, whichever is the later.

## Oil tanks

OK provided that:

- its capacity does not exceed 3,500 litres
- it is not higher than three metres
- it is not nearer the highway than the original building

## Garages

OK provided that:

- the rules relating to extensions generally are complied with
- no part of the building is within five metres of the residence itself (carports are treated the same as garages).

### Driveways
Only permitted without permission if they give access to an unclassified road. Otherwise a full application and probably the consent of the Highways Authority will be necessary.

### TV aerials
No planning permission is required, but in respect of radio masts a formal application for permission will be necessary.

### Part II in further detail
Remember that Part II of the GDO relates to minor operations. This is something of a catch-all exception and covers quite an array of development/activity.

### Walls and fences
No permission is required provided the wall or fence in question is less than two metres in height (or one metre if it faces the highway). This therefore covers the erection, construction, maintenance, improvement and alteration of walls, fences **and** gates.

### Hedges
see Walls and Fences.

### External painting
Again no permission is required provided the painting is not an advertisement. If you live in a leasehold property however, there may well be covenants which prevent external decoration without the consent of the freeholder.

### Internal alterations
Again no permission unless the work relates to a change of use (see later).

### Routine maintenance
This does not require planning permission. Therefore work such as stone-cladding, pebble dashing, repointing, and fitting shutters are all OK, even if the external appearance of the house is altered. However, if you live in a conservation area, the rules will be different. Part 4 of the GDO deals with

temporary buildings. This exemption is basically to cover the erection/installation of temporary structures which are ancillary to the main building. For example if you are having major structural work done on your property, the contractor may erect a temporary site office. This is quite acceptable provided it is removed at the end of the job and that planning permission has been granted for the main work.

## Applying for planning permission

If your proposed development is not caught by the GDO a full application for planning permission will have to be submitted to your LPA. The procedure is somewhat mystical and tales abound at the blackballing tactics of some planning councillors. In fact many more applications are approved than refused and the decision-making process is much less arbitrary than many would have you believe. Well-advised, researched and planned applications are naturally much more likely to pass through the system than cobbled-together, over-imaginative ones. It may be a good idea to have an informal discussion with a local planning officer before your plans are submitted. Whatever you are told will be off the record and not binding in any way, but at least it will give some guidance.

## The application

You must obtain the correct forms and pay the appropriate fee to your LPA. The time for consideration of your application does not start until these have been submitted to the LPA. Accompanying the application must be an ownership certificate. This is a legal requirement confirming that at the date of submission you are either the owner, or make the application with the current owner's consent.

## Notification

Once all the paperwork has been submitted, your application is placed in the planning register. This is a public document which all members of the general public are entitled to inspect. The application may also be publicised by a site display or by notifying your neighbours. Newspaper notices will be placed in special cases, for example where local environmental issues are raised.

## Objections

Anyone can object to a planning application. Neighbours or those objecting to a site display have twenty-one days to do so from the date of notification. In the case of newspaper ads, the period for objection is fourteen days. The planning officer concerned must put these objections to the committee - the complainant is not allowed to make oral representations himself. Planning officers are used to hearing complaints so they will use their experience to assess the merits of each one. Moaning neighbours for example, who are simply being obstructive for the sake of it, are unlikely to have their complaints taken seriously.

**Time-scale**
Applications have to be considered within eight weeks of submission although decisions are usually reached within six. If you do not hear within eight weeks you can probably assume that your application has been turned down.

**The decision**
There are three decisions:

- refusal.
- approval without conditions.
- approval subject to conditions specified in writing by the LPA.

The reasons for refusal must also be communicated in writing. Armed with these reasons you should consult with your architect to ascertain what amendments will be necessary if you are likely to be successful at a fresh application. Do not give up hope (yet!). The conditions attached to the grant of permission can be wide-ranging and include for example the type of stone to be used. Again be guided by a professional as he may be able to strike a deal with the planning officer once permission has been granted. Eventually a compromise which is acceptable to both parties may be reached.

**Validity**
Planning permission is valid for five years from the date it was granted. But this rule is not hard and fast and may ultimately be in the discretion of the LPA in certain cases.

**Appeals**
So the plans for an Olympic-sized swimming pool are turned down. What do you do? You could on the advice of your architect, submit a fresh application for permission. However if this proves fruitless, then you must appeal to the Secretary of State for the Environment. This is likely to be an expensive process and of course you may be receiving advice from a professional who has a vested interest, so beware. If you go ahead, the appeal must be lodged in the correct format within six months of your receipt of the original decision. Accompanying reasons for the appeal and evidence you will rely on must also be sent. Through delegated powers, the Secretary of State hands the appeal to

a Planning Inspector. The Inspector has a wide range of powers to assist him with your appeal and he can ask the interested parties for additional evidence etc. The appeal itself however is heard at a Public Inquiry.

At the Inquiry the Inspector has a discretion to conduct the appeal very much as he pleases and to hear objections/evidence from whomsoever he deems relevant. It is worth bearing in mind that at appeal the original decision is "at large". This means that in addition to allowing your appeal, he can also uphold the original decision or impose **more** onerous conditions. Again the decision of the Inspector must be communicated to you in writing. The above is really only a brief summary of what is involved at a planning appeal. It can be a time consuming, expensive and very stressful exercise, so be prepared to listen to people who are not as close to the appeal as you are. We are all guilty at times of only seeing things from a very personal angle. If we stepped back, the futility of certain applications may be obvious.

### Enforcing planning regulations

Build at your peril! The principal weapon of the LPA is the **enforcement notice**. There are two limits which have to be complied with. If your development without permission includes the following:

* building.
* change of use to a single dwelling-house or,
* a failure to comply with a prohibition to do (ii), then the LPA has four years to issue an enforcement notice. In all other cases where planning regulations have been breached, the period is ten years. So if you built your own garage five years ago without planning permission - you've got away with it!

The Enforcement Notice itself is a legal document and should include the following:

* details about the alleged breach.
* the steps to be taken to remedy the breach by making the development comply with the terms of any planning permission granted, or by restoring the land to its previous condition.
* details of dates and periods for compliance with the Notice.

You can appeal against an enforcement notice, but such an appeal is probably beyond the terms of this book. Be very sure of your ground before appealing. Failure to comply with an Enforcement Notice is serious. The LPA can take

**criminal** proceedings against you. If the case proceeds to a Crown Court, the judge could award an unlimited fine against you. Ultimately the Enforcement Notice may empower the LPA to demolish your development - for many this would be the most serious punishment of all.

## 4.2 CHANGE OF USE

This is something of a strange issue to many people. In essence planning permission is required if there has been a material change of use of your property. During the recent recessionary times, many people who were made redundant set up small businesses from home, often not realising that planning permission was required. Every case will turn on its own facts when the question of materiality is raised. Some cases are obvious. If you start using your garage to service and maintain vehicles on a commercial basis, planning permission is required, even if no building work as such is necessary. But of course this is only fair - who would like to live next door to a noisy workshop, lewd calendars and a stream of visiting traffic? A writer who works from home or a freelance small-scale hairdresser probably would not need planning permission, but a chiropodist advertising her services would. The new use must therefore be substantially different from the previous use. If you have any questions relating to your proposed business or if you think that a neighbour has materially changed the use of his property without permission, speak with a local planning officer.

The GDO does permit certain changes of use without the need for planning permission. Types of use have been categorised according to the Use Classes Order. Thus:

**Class A1** - general non-food shops.
**Class A2** - financial, professional services.
**Class A3** - premises where food and drink is sold.
**Class B1** - businesses and offices.
**Class B2** - general industrial.
**Class C1** - hotels and hostels.
**Class C3** - dwelling houses.
**Class D2** - assembly and leisure.

Under the GDO it is permissible to change the use of premises within the same use class. Therefore it would be possible to change a solicitor's office (A2) to that of an insurance broker without the need for planning permission. But if the solicitor's office already classified as (A2) were to be converted into an ice-cream parlour (A3), permission would be required.

## 4.3  TREE PRESERVATION ORDERS (TPO)

LPA's are under a statutory obligation "in the interest of amenity" to identify trees or woodlands etc. to prevent them from being felled, uprooted or pruned. The procedure for so doing is the Tree Preservation Order. A breach of a TPO is a criminal offence. Once a tree has been highlighted, the LPA must serve a notice on you giving twenty-eight days to object and make your representations. The objections must be in writing with evidence in support. Only fairly extreme grounds are likely to prevent the TPO being confirmed. Once made the Order is binding on all purchasers of your land, whether they have knowledge of it or not. Ignorance of the TPO is no excuse if you cut down the tree. If you feel that a TPO should be lifted, you must follow the procedure laid down by your LPA. If you live in a conservation area, try to control your chain saw urges until you have spoken with the LPA as a rash cut could land you in the same hot water as if a TPO had been breached.

## 4.4  BUILDING REGULATIONS

Building regulations are a quite separate issue from planning permission. It is the function of building regulations to ensure that your development is properly built and structurally sound. In many cases where planning permission is not required, you will have to comply with buildings regulations. The regulations relate to items such as ventilation, chimneys and flues, refuse disposal, sanitary provision, structural stability and insulation. The regulations themselves may be quite onerous and to the inexperienced, may read like double dutch. In most cases you will have instructed a qualified architect or experienced builder who will be able to guide you through the maze. If you are a budding DIYer, contact the local authority for advice!

### Procedure

Your builder submits a series of written notices to the district surveyor including a set of plans plus details of the proposed materials. If the district surveyor is unhappy with the detail of your plans then he must give written reasons for his objections. You can appeal in much the same way to the Secretary of State for the Environment, but this would only be in the most extreme of cases. Normally a workable compromise is reached. Once approved but before work starts you or your builder must then serve a Notice of Commencement on the district surveyor. As the work progresses a local authority buildings inspector will check that the construction complies with the plans and specifications. Inspections are important so keep checking with your builder that too much work has not been completed before the next inspection. The inspector is quite at liberty to halt or demolish work with which he is not entirely happy.

**Breaches of building regulations**
In many respects, these are just as serious as those where planning permission has not been sought. You could fall foul of the criminal law, be fined and have your property made the subject of a demolition order. In many cases if you have really acted in good faith and in ignorance of building regulations, approval can be issued retrospectively provided adequate materials have been used and the structure erected to a high enough standard.

## 4.5 FOOTNOTE
For many, the prospects of having to comply with both planning and building requirements is too much. But a word of caution. If you go ahead with your proposed development without having followed the correct procedures, be prepared for the consequences. As with so much in life the benefits of corner cutting in the short-term can have drastic effects later on.

# Chapter 5

## Dealing with the utility companies

If you live on a paradise island with a plentiful supply of fresh drinking water, an efficient jungle communications system and are quite happy to live by candlelight during the hours of darkness, pass on to Chapter 6. If not, then regrettably to live to any kind of standard, you will have to pay for the services of telecommunications, electricity, water and gas. We simply do not have a choice here and perhaps with these industries more than any other, the feeling of "them and us" still pervades. Because we cannot live without water/electricity etc., in a sense we have to be bound by each supplier's terms and conditions. However, with increased consumer awareness and empowerment, things are changing slowly. Parliament too has responded - ongoing privatisations and the Competition and Service (Utilities) Act 1992 provide service standards and a defined complaints procedure. Recently, because British Gas received a record number of complaints, the Government's ultimate sanction of removing its Charter Mark, came in for consideration.

## 5.1 TELEPHONE

British Telecom (BT) has lost its monopoly. Whilst other telephone service providers have not flooded the market as anticipated, nevertheless, there is now room for healthy competition. Once you sign up a supply contract with BT or Mercury, the usual rules of contract law apply. But the supplier's principal advantage over its subscribers is that your telephone can be disconnected if the bill is not paid. Unlike consumer credit agreements there is no period of grace to pay the bill. Technically it is payable on demand. A reminder and final notice will be sent, but questions answered later!

### Complaining

In terms of an excessive bill, to avoid being disconnected, it is probably advisable to pay at least the part which you agree with. You should then, ideally in writing, complain to the supplier concerned. It will check the line, your equipment and any other factors which could have given rise to erroneous readings. Most subscribers are now on digital exchanges which produce itemised bills (for calls of more than a certain length). These should go some way in alleviating any problems about billing. However, if you reach deadlock, then you really only have two options. Firstly to sue using the small claims procedure of the county court (see Chapter 8) or secondly to involve The Office of Telecommunications (Oftel, see Useful Addresses). Whilst everyone is entitled to their day in court, for most disputes, the county court is probably not the most suitable forum. It can be a quite cumbersome and time-consuming process. It should therefore be seen as something of a last resort or to be used in the more complex cases.

Oftel is the industry watchdog and has a monitoring and enforcement role to play over BT, Mercury, mobile network operators and local cable companies. In fact, any organisation which has a telecommunications licence. It is not dissimilar to an Ombudsman but it is a government department - much like the Office of Fair Trading. Oftel handles many complaints - in 1993 it received over 23,000, the bulk of which related to bills. Oftel has a range of functions, but for the homeowner, it is its role as an arbitrator of complaints about services and apparatus which is most beneficial. The Director-General at Oftel has adequate powers for dealing with complaints. He can demand that the service provider gives him all the evidence relating to the dispute and to force that company to be bound by his decision. Also if the licence holders persistently breach the conditions of their licence, Oftel can make orders which can be enforced through the civil courts. A recent good example of Oftel's powers can be seen in respect of the charge levied for use of the Directory Enquiries service. Oftel intervened on behalf of the consumer and slashed the charge of this service by almost 50%.

## BT service standards

Under the Citizens' Charter, BT has certain standards which it has to attain. All of us have doubtless reported a fault and waited for days for an engineer to call. Or we may have waited in and taken time off work only for BT not to turn up. Now BT is obliged to pay up to £1000 in compensation if you can prove a financial loss which is directly attributable to their failure to reach a target. Alternatively, and of more relevance to most subscribers, is the fact that you can claim one month's line rental reimbursement for each day that you are without a telephone, provided:

- BT has failed to attend a fixed appointment.
- if having reported a fault, BT fails to repair this fault by the end of the next working day.

The key to effective complaining can be summarised:

- always be reasonable.
- try not to lose your temper.
- always confirm in writing.
- collect as much supporting evidence as possible.
- be prepared to consider the broad picture - what options are open to resolve your dispute?
- never fight solely on a point of principle.

- notify early.
- if you have to resort to civil litigation measures be prepared for a long wait (see Appendix 1 for an example of a draft Particulars of Claim).

## 5.2 ELECTRICITY
The electricity industry was privatised in 1989 following the introduction of the Electricity Act. But although privatised, all suppliers are still bound by statutory obligations - i.e. certain standards have to be complied with. In addition you have rights in both nuisance and negligence against suppliers if you or your property rights have been infringed.

### Offer
The regulatory body for the industry is an independent government organisation called the Office of Electricity Regulation (Offer). It is quasi-governmental and is run and constituted in much the same way as Oftel. It has two principal aims, to protect customers and to promote competition. In terms of prices, Offer reviews the levels set by suppliers every few years. For the customer, Offer has introduced guaranteed performance standards for each of the local electricity companies, some of which can be enforced by financial penalty. In 1994 Offer received nearly 11,000 customer complaints, the bulk of which related to billing. If you have a dispute and fail to pay the final demand, the ultimate sanction is to disconnect your supply. As a condition of its licence, each supplier is required to operate a Code of Practice for customers who have problems paying the bills. Since the introduction of the Code far fewer homes have been disconnected. In total, the figure for 1993/94 was just under 3,000.

In any event disconnection can only follow adequate warning and opportunity to state your case. Your supply cannot be disconnected if the disputed bill was an estimate or if the bill has not been paid due to a mistake. In terms of challenging a meter reading, you must contact your local supplier and give reasons why you think that the bill is on the high side. They will then send an engineer to check the apparatus. There may be a charge for this service - but if there is a problem, then the cost will be refunded. If this fails to produce a satisfactory outcome or if you do not accept their evidence, you can refer the complaint to Offer directly. As with telephone disputes, court action should really only be seen as a last resort. Offer has wide ranging powers to compel suppliers to put matters straight.

### Guaranteed service standards
Perhaps Offer's greatest contribution to improving the lot of the domestic electricity consumer has been the introduction of service standards. The

principal areas are shown in table 3, together with the current compensation levels. Obviously, the compensation payable under the guaranteed standards cannot be sought where delays/failures are due to severe weather or other matters over which the supplier has no control.

| SERVICE | PERFORMANCE LEVEL | PENALTY PAYMENT |
|---|---|---|
| Restoring electricity supplies after faults | 24 hours | £40 domestic customers £100 non-domestic. Plus £20 for each further 12 hours |
| Providing supply and meter | Within 3 working days for domestic customers (and 5 working days for non-domestic customers) | £40 domestic customers £100 non-domestic |
| Estimating charges | Within 10 working days for simple jobs or 20 working days for most others | £40 |
| Notice of supply interruption | At least 2 days | £20 domestic customers £40 non-domestic customers |
| Meter problems | Visit or reply within 10 working days | £20 |
| Charges and payment queries | A substantive reply within 10 working days | £20 |
| Appointments | All appointments to visit on a day must be kept | £20 |
| Payments owed under Standards | Write to customer within 10 working days of failure | £20 |

Table 3. Guaranteed standards of performance.

As well as guaranteed performance standards, Offer has introduced overall standards which suppliers must strive to attain. Although compensation is not payable to an aggrieved customer, such standards are definitely a step in the right direction. Overall standards include:

• a minimum percentage of all customer letters to be replied to within ten working days.

- a minimum percentage of customers who have been cut off for non-payment to be reconnected before the end of the working day after they have paid the bill.
- minimum percentage of voltage faults to be corrected within six months
- ensuring that the supplier obtains a meter reading at least once a year.

### Power failures

Table 3 shows the level of compensation payable in the event of a power cut. However, this is merely part of Offer's scheme. If the supplier has been negligent and you have suffered provable loss then your claim is unlimited. Of course this is more likely to affect businesses where production lines etc. may be halted. Many companies take out a business interruption policy of insurance to protect against such an eventuality. Also, as a consumer proving negligence could be a tricky and costly exercise involving detailed experts' reports. If you do have a sizeable claim, then you really ought to be guided by a solicitor.

### Breaking into your home

In cases of emergency an electricity supply company can break into your home at any time to effect immediate repairs/preventive measures. Your home should be left reasonably secure afterwards. In all other cases, the supplier can use reasonable force to gain entry only under the protection of a warrant. Such force can only be applied after you have been given at least twenty-four hours notice and you have persistently refused to allow access.

### Stealing electricity

Stealing or abstracting electricity is an offence contrary to the Theft Act 1968. In the past a whole plethora of devices may have been used to either jam, block or otherwise force a meter to give erroneous readings. Many may see little harm in such action - after all the electricity companies do make so much money. In fact, the courts view the offence very seriously and any use, waste or diversion of electricity will suffice. In a case in 1980 a man fitted a device which caused his meter to give a false reading. The High Court Judge sent a strong message that penalties should carry a deterrent element and the offender in question was sent to prison.

### 5.3 GAS

Much of what has been said about electricity and telephones, also applies to gas supply. Although British Gas was sold off by the Government in 1986, competition for consumers has been slow to come to the market. In a sense a form of monopoly is therefore still in existence and because British Gas is no longer a publicly owned company, removing its Citizens' Charter Mark is the only way government can express its disapproval of the way the company is being run.

## Complaining

Your complaint may relate to the bill, an appliance or the service being provided. In the first instance it should be to your regional British Gas office. If this fails to satisfy, the complaint should be referred to the local Gas Consumers Council (GCC, see Useful Addresses). The GCC was set up by the Gas Act 1986 to consider any complaint about supply and service against members of the gas industry. Currently it handles a record number about rude staff, poor service, misleading accounts and the non-answering of telephones. Whilst the GCC can respond and make recommendations its decisions cannot be enforced. For some complaints (supply and bills) the GCC can refer on to the Office of Gas Supply (Ofgas, see Useful Addresses).

In 1993 British Gas disconnected 16,000 domestic supplies, the bulk in relation to non-payment of bills. There may also be a disconnection and reconnection fee to consider. Ofgas carefully monitors the operation of the legally enforceable disconnection procedures which safeguard customers who have difficulty in paying their gas bills. In terms of disconnection British Gas must give twenty-eight days from the date of the original bill and then a further seven days [written notice] before disconnection. You should be given every opportunity to pay the bill, or a proportion of the bill and be offered alternative methods of payment. Disconnection should be seen as a last resort. If the dispute is about the size of your bill, consider paying the proportion which you feel is reasonable. Then either challenge British Gas or refer the matter on to the GCC for a consideration.

## Forcing entry

The same rules apply as for Electricity but forced entry may be more common because of the greater risk of fire and explosion.

## 5.4 WATER

Again the Competition and Service (Utilities) Act 1992 was instrumental in reforming the accountability and complaints procedures associated with the water and sewerage companies. The Office of Water Services (Ofwat, see Useful Addresses) is responsible for making sure that these companies give good quality water at a fair price and with efficient services. Ofwat has 10 regional Customer Service Committees (CSC's) which in 1993-94 received over 14,000 complaints. The bulk of these complaints related to bills and overcharging. Ofwat is also responsible for the approval of each supplier's

Code of Practice. If you choose to have a water meter, your water company should offer a reasonably priced scheme. The water industry also has a Guaranteed Standards Scheme which offers customers compensation if not met. At present the following standards are guaranteed:

- keeping appointments (or cancellation with at least twenty-four hours' notice).
- responding to complaints within ten working days.
- warning you of planned interruptions to the supply which are going to exceed four hours.
- making a payment if your property is flooded from the communal sewer.

If either of these standards are not attained you will be entitled to a cash sum of £10. During 1993-94, 11,388 compensation payments were made totalling over £214,000. The maximum sum payable for severe flooding incidents is currently £1000. In terms of a complaint, this should first be made in writing to the water or sewerage company concerned. If this fails to bring you the desired response you should complain to your local CSC. Ideally you should detail the history of your complaint and supply supporting evidence. An indication of the response you are seeking would also be helpful.

The CSC will then make recommendations to the company concerned to put right your problem. Although not binding, in most cases the recommendations are accepted and acted upon. If you are unhappy with the way the CSC handled your complaint your redress is to the Director General of Water Services. In most cases Ofwat will achieve a satisfactory outcome to your complaint. You can assist by making your case as clear as possible and providing all **relevant** evidence. It cannot however handle complaints about:

- water for which the National Rivers Authority has responsibility.
- matters which can be taken to arbitration.
- matters which should be dealt with in a court of law.

## Disconnection
Your supply may be disconnected in two cases. Firstly if your bill is unpaid and you have been sent seven days' notice of the intention to disconnect. And secondly if it is necessary to effect repairs to the system. If your supply is interrupted you will be entitled to compensation under the Guaranteed Standards Scheme. In an emergency the supply company could force entry into your home. In all other cases if you refuse to grant permission, the

company concerned would need to seek a warrant to enter. A refusal to comply with this could be a contempt of court.

## Drinking water

The Drinking Water Inspectorate in England and Wales is responsible for ensuring that the water companies supply water which is safe to drink and complies with the Water Supply (Water Quality) Regulations. It carries out over three million tests each year. Local environmental health officers also keep an eye on the water quality in your area. If there is the risk of infection, it is the Inspectorate which advises to boil the water etc. It may also recommend prosecution. If you suffer loss, perhaps from a stomach disorder which is attributable to the company concerned not meeting its statutory requirements you can sue in negligence in the civil courts. It is unlikely that you would be the only one affected in your area so liaise closely with local environmental health officers to ascertain whether any prosecutions are in the offing. If your loss is more than £275 you could also claim under the Consumer Protection Act. Lead in the water supply has been a problem for some time. The reduction of lead levels at consumers' taps may require the replacement of your plumbing - this would be at your expense.

# Chapter 6

## Letting out your home

Over recent years, the property market has stagnated. Many homeowners who would otherwise have moved on and up the ladder, have had to look at alternatives because of the problems of negative equity and unemployment. One alternative may be to let their homes and in turn rent themselves. Indeed lettings companies are suffering from a shortage of good properties for an ever increasing list of potential tenants. Letting and managing companies have prospered during the property slump. Whatever the reasons for letting your home, doing it properly is an absolute must. If all the formalities are not complied with, you could give your tenants security of tenure making subsequent eviction potentially very difficult. This chapter is not intended to be a comprehensive guide to residential tenancy law - it does however cover the principal areas of concern to the landlord who lets his property under an Assured Shorthold Tenancy Agreement (AST). You may choose to let your home through an agent. If this is the case, there is a natural feeling that you can let them worry about the law and technicalities. To a degree this is certainly very true but there are many unscrupulous, unprofessional and inexperienced agents currently in the market. It is therefore critical in protecting your long-term security that you know at least something of the operation of an AST. If you are to let, always look for an agent who is a member of the Association of Residential Letting Agents (ARLA, see Useful Addresses). Members must have a minimum of two years' expertise, provide separate accounts for clients' money, carry professional indemnity insurance and operate from business premises. A letting agent will really only find you a tenant, draw up the papers and collect the rent. For this they will generally charge around ten per cent of the rental for the term of the tenancy. Many agents also offer a full management service, taking care of your home for another five to seven and a half per cent on top of the letting fee. They should check on your property two to four times a year and advise you of any problems, potential or actual. They may also advise on possession proceedings if necessary.

## 6.1 ASSURED SHORTHOLD TENANCIES (AST)

The AST was introduced by the Housing Act 1988 and has today become the most widespread type of private residential tenancy agreement. It is beneficial to both landlord and tenant. For the landlord because the tenant never gets security of tenure thereby entitling him to guaranteed possession of his property, and for the tenant because the property is let at a market rate and he is entitled to exclusive possession of the property for the duration of the agreement. Exclusive possession is an important element of an AST and one which potential landlords should be fully aware of. Simply, once you have let your property, you have no right to go into your home for any reason without the express consent of your tenant. So popping in to collect stray post whilst the tenant is at work is definitely not on and could entitle the tenant to go to court and claim damages. An AST is an assured tenancy which:

- is for a minimum term of six months.
- contains no power for the landlord to terminate it during the first six months.
- was preceded by giving a notice in the correct format (S.20 Housing Act) to the tenant.

These three conditions are essential in distinguishing an AST from an assured tenancy. If not complied with, an assured tenancy may be created giving the tenant full security of tenure. A tenancy is *assured* provided the dwelling house is let as a separate dwelling and all of the following requirements are met:

- the tenant or each of joint tenants is an individual (excludes letting to companies).
- the tenant occupies the property as his only or principal home.
- the tenancy is not specifically excluded by other provisions of the Housing Act 1988 (e.g. tenancies entered into before 15th January 1989, high value property tenancies at a low rent, business tenancies, agricultural tenancies, holiday lettings and tenancies where the landlord lives in the same building).

Prior to the grant of the AST a formal notice under S.20 **must** be given to the tenant. In essence it is to inform the tenant that he will not acquire security of tenure. It **must** be in writing in the correct format. An example is seen below.

## HOUSING ACT 1988
## Section 20

## NOTICE OF AN ASSURED SHORTHOLD TENANCY

*Please write clearly in black ink.*

If there is anything you do not understand you should get advice from a solicitor or a Citizens' Advice Bureau, before you agree to the tenancy.

The landlord must give this notice to the tenant before an assured shorthold tenancy is granted. It does not commit the tenant to take the tenancy.

**THIS DOCUMENT IS IMPORTANT, KEEP IT IN A SAFE PLACE.**

To:          ................................................................

             ................................................................

1.  You are proposing to take a tenancy of the dwelling known as:

             ................................................................

             ................................................................

             ................................................................

from the            day of                19
to the              day of                19

2.  This notice is to tell you that your tenancy is to be an *assured shorthold tenancy*. Provided you keep to the terms of the tenancy, you are entitled to remain in the dwelling for at least the first six months of the fixed period agreed at the start of the tenancy. At the end of this period, depending on the terms of the tenancy, the landlord may have the right to repossession if he/she wants.

3.  The rent for this tenancy is the rent we have agreed. However, you have the right to apply to a rent assessment committee for a determination of the rent which the committee considers might reasonably be obtained under the tenancy. If the committee considers (i) that there is a sufficient number of similar properties in the locality let on assured tenancies and that (ii) the rent we have agreed is significantly higher than the rent which might reasonably be obtained having regard to the level of rents for other assured tenancies in the locality, it will determine a rent for the tenancy. That rent will be the legal maximum you can be required to pay from the date the committee directs. If the rent includes a payment for council tax, the rent determined by the committee will be inclusive of council tax.

To be signed by the landlord or his/her agent (someone acting for him/her). If there are joint landlords each must sign, unless one signs on behalf of the rest with their agreement.

**Signed**:                     ....................................................

**Name(s) of
landlord(s)**:                  ....................................................

                                ....................................................

**Address of
landlord(s)**:                  ....................................................

                                ....................................................

                                ....................................................

**Telephone**:                  ....................................................

**If signed by agent, name and address of agent**

                                ....................................................

                                ....................................................

                                ....................................................

**Telephone**:            .............................. **Date**: ............

You should check that the commencement date of the term does not precede the date of the grant of the tenancy. If the start and end dates are specified, check that a clear six month period is granted. If the term is expressed to run "from" a specified date rather than "from and including", the specified date is excluded from the calculation. For example, a tenancy granted "from 30th June 1996 until 31st December 1996" could be for less than six months. It is worth noting that you cannot grant an AST to an existing assured tenant in an attempt to undermine that tenant's position who does have security of tenure. The AST could be given under the correct procedure but would have no legally binding effect on the assured tenant.

### Market rate, rent and rent books, council tax

Under an AST, the property can only be let at the market rate. The landlord cannot raise the rent on a whim throughout the duration of the agreement. The tenant however can complain to a local rent assessment committee if the rent is too high. The tenant must make his application in the correct form and ask the committee to assess a reasonable rent. In essence it will look at similar properties let in the area to consider the market rate. The rent which the committee decides upon is binding immediately.

The Landlord and Tenant Act 1985 details when a rent book must be given. As most AST rent payments are made on a monthly basis, there is **no** requirement to have a rent book. There is however a strict obligation to provide a rent book to tenants where the rent is payable weekly. The liability for council tax falls on the person in occupation of the "dwelling" in question, i.e. the tenant. The rule does not apply however to houses in multiple occupation, for example large houses sub-divided into bedsits, or where the landlord lives in. In such cases the landlord will be responsible for paying the council tax (see also Chapter 11).

### Insurance and mortgage

It is normal for the landlord to insure the buildings and his contents. The tenant has an option to take out additional contents insurance to protect his own belongings. You must advise your insurers in advance of the tenancy. If you fail to notify they may refuse to pay out should you need to make a claim. The same applies to your mortgage - it will be a condition of your mortgage that you get permission before letting.

### Sub-letting

AST's usually prohibit tenants sub-letting the whole or any part of your premises. If the tenant does sub-let, contrary to the agreement, the rights of the sub-tenant will come to an end at the same time as the original tenant. Breach of such an agreement may also give you as the landlord the opportunity to repossess under one of the discretionary grounds (see later).

### Deposit

It is normal to take a deposit to provide security against non-payment of rent and/or damage to the property. The deposit may be one month, two months or six weeks depending upon the value of the property which effectively you will be protecting. The agreement should state the circumstances in which you as landlord may retain the deposit and when it is repayable. Many tenants abuse the deposit system by refusing to make the last months' payment knowing that the landlord (or his agent) already holds money. Therefore a failure to take a large enough deposit at the outset could be problematic later on if the property is left in a poor condition.

## Break clauses

With an AST, the tenant is effectively locked into a fixed-term contract for the full term. For example if you let your property for twelve months but the tenant wants to leave after eight he will still be liable for the outstanding four months' rent (unless you come to an arrangement with him or you can find another tenant). A break clause however is a term in the agreement allowing either the landlord or tenant to terminate early (but they can only be effective in agreements of at least six months). If either party terminates the agreement in accordance with the break clause, then he will not be liable for the outstanding rent.

## Leasehold property

If you live in a leasehold property (usually a flat) there will be an express covenant prohibiting letting of the property. Of course what the freeholder does not know about cannot be a problem, but you should be aware that if there are problems, the freeholder may seek to forfeit your leasehold agreement (but probably unlikely).

## References

Two references are usually required - one in respect of the proposed tenant's character and one from his bank. You could also seek a reference from the tenant's employers.

## Guarantors

If you are less than satisfied as to the tenant's ability to keep up the rent payments, consider guaranteeing them. A guarantor effectively agrees to meet the rental and other financial obligations of the tenant and can be sued for a failure to do so. Obviously you must be satisfied that the guarantor is financially solvent.

## Stamp duty

Stamp duty is a tax payable on certain tenancy agreements. However it is only likely to be an issue for the tenant and many agreements are issued quite ignorant of the requirement to pay tax. The amount of duty payable by the tenant will depend upon the duration of the tenancy and the amount of rent payable. Stamp duty on agreements of less than twelve months is nominal. A failure to stamp the agreement makes it unenforceable in court. However if court proceedings do follow then you can subsequently have the agreement stamped. The duty payable will have accrued interest and in some cases, the Inland Revenue has a discretion to charge double duty. If in doubt, speak with the Inland Revenue Stamp Office (see Useful Addresses).

## Inventories
A detailed inventory should be taken before the tenant moves in. He should be given the opportunity to comment and to agree on what is contained in it. At the conclusion a further inventory should be taken. Without such a laborious exercise you may be in a weak position if you are seeking to withhold some or all of the security deposit.

## Expiry of an AST
One of the principal benefits of the AST, is that on expiry of the term the landlord has an automatic right to possession of his home, **provided** a S.21 Notice has been served on the tenant at *least* 2 months before the expiry date (see below).

---

### Housing Act 1988

#### Section 21

#### Assured shorthold tenancy notice requiring possession

To:       Duncan Callow [name of tenant]
Of:       22 Acacia Avenue [address of tenant]

From:   Pamela Beachbabe [name of landlord]
Of:       Malibu Beach, Calif. USA [address of landlord]

I hereby give you notice that I require possession of the dwelling house known as 22 Acacia Avenue

On:       31st December 1996 [date of expiry of notice] by virtue of Section 21 of the Housing Act 1988

Dated:

Signed: Pamela Beachbabe

---

Note that the two month notice period is the minimum - many landlords will serve the Section 21 Notice at the beginning of the agreement so as not to subsequently forget. If this Notice is served late, i.e. less than two months before the due date then it is not effective for two months from its date of service - for example if Pamela Beachbabe served the Notice on the date when six months of a six month agreement is up (and not within the first four months), then Duncan Callow effectively has an eight month AST. If the S.21 Notice is properly served and in time and the tenant refuses to vacate, then the landlord is entitled to seek an automatic court order for possession.

You can let the tenant stay in possession. Provided the parties are the same, a new tenancy of the same property will be deemed to be a shorthold unless the landlord serves a notice to the contrary. A periodic tenancy is then created and the term thereafter need not be for a minimum of six months. If this is allowed to happen, then a notice under S.21(4) must eventually be served under a periodic tenancy. The landlord must give at least two months' notice to take effect on the last day of a period of the tenancy.

If there has been a change in the identity of the tenant or landlord on a renewal, the new tenancy cannot be or be deemed to be shorthold. In such a case, a new tenancy must be entered into complying with all the usual shorthold requirements. But if you are contemplating a new tenant, you can give him the benefit of a deemed shorthold provided he is first made a tenant under the expiring agreement! The new tenancy will then be a deemed shorthold as the new landlord and tenant will be identical to those under the old lease (even if this is a rather backdoor (but legal) way of doing so).

## Repossession of your home

Most AST's run smoothly and provided the S.21 Notice is served in time and in the correct form, you should take repossession on the due date. However there can be problems - either the tenant refuses to leave or he has failed to pay the rent or the property may have been seriously damaged or "illegal" tenants etc. shipped in. The general rule is that you cannot evict without a court order, however serious the circumstances. Repossession should be carried out by a solicitor well-versed in such practices and who can advise on the enforcement of your rights in general. However there are three steps to be considered:

* notice of proceedings.
* issue of proceedings.
* enforcement of a court order.

Section 8 of the Housing Act 1988 sets out the procedure which you must follow if the tenant breaks the terms of the agreement. Notice must first be served in the prescribed form specifying the grounds upon which possession will be sought. A S.8 Notice in the incorrect form could render the whole process unenforceable. The Notice must be served two weeks before proceedings proper are issued. The grounds for possession are listed in Schedule 2 of the Housing Act 1988. Schedule 2 is sub-divided into Part I where a court **must** order possession (the mandatory grounds) and Part II where a court **may** order possession (the discretionary grounds).

**Part I** - *Mandatory*

**Ground 1**: owner occupier.
**Ground 2**: mortgagee exercising power of sale.
**Ground 3**: out of season holiday let.
**Ground 4**: out of term student let.
**Ground 5**: religious minister's home.
**Ground 6**: demolition or reconstruction of the property.
**Ground 7**: death.
**Ground 8**: substantial rent arrears - thirteen weeks if payable weekly or three months if payable monthly. In addition, the rent must be in arrears at both the date of the service of the S.8 Notice and at the date of the hearing.

**Part II** - *Discretionary*

**Ground 9**: if the landlord can prove suitable alternative accommodation is available at the date of possession.
**Ground 10**: rent arrears if:

* some rent is owing on the date possession proceedings are commenced.
* some rent was owing at the date of service of the S.8 Notice.

**Ground 11**: persistent delay in paying rent.
**Ground 12**: breach of covenant, e.g. not to have pets.
**Ground 13**: waste or neglect of the property.
**Ground 14**: nuisance caused to adjoining neighbours.
**Ground 15**: damage to furniture arising from neglect.
**Ground 16**: a former employee of the landlord.

These grounds have deliberately not been discussed in detail, but merely included to show the diverse range open to the landlord. Grounds 8,10 and 11 are subject to the right of the tenant to withhold rent in the event that he has been forced to carry out essential repairs which are the landlord's responsibility. If the tenant is in arrears, it will be usual for the landlord to seek repossession. However, if the tenant is good for the money and has a regular income etc., you could instead sue for the arrears as damages, via an ordinary civil claim, thereby retaining the tenancy agreement.

If you are seeking possession under Grounds 1,3,4 and 5, a new accelerated procedure is available. In all other cases the landlord must bring an ordinary action for possession through the county court. If a tenant is in breach of a covenant or is in arrears of rent and possession proceedings have been commenced, any future monies paid by the tenant should be as "mesne profits". Accepting "rent" may indicate that you have waived the breach and prejudiced your chances of reclaiming possession.

## 6.2 LANDLORD'S REPAIRING OBLIGATIONS

A landlord will always be responsible for repairs to the structure and exterior of any property he lets on agreements of less than seven years' duration. He will also be responsible for ensuring adequate water, electricity, sewage, gas and refuse collection facilities. In turn the tenant must keep the property in relatively good order. This does not mean that it has to be redecorated and steam cleaned before he hands the keys back. "Clean and tidy" is a somewhat subjective concept - some of us may live like barbarians whilst others are obsessive about cleanliness. Because of the potential problems, the standard to be applied is one of objective reasonableness. In other words if a judge were to hear the circumstances of the case, what could he reasonably expect of the parties to the tenancy agreement.

Security deposits are important to protect you against unfair wear and tear. Every case will turn on its facts, but if your new Axminster has had more than its fair share of cigarette burns, then it may be reasonable to insist on a replacement - a threadbare old rug would be much more difficult to justify replacing. Consider instead contract cleaning etc. If you do reach an impasse and either the security deposit is insufficient to cover remedial costs or the tenant will not accept the defects, be prepared to consult an independent expert, e.g. the Textile Services Association (see Useful Addresses). The "loser" will have to pay for the ultimate costs of such a report.

## 6.3 RESIDENT LANDLORD/LICENCE AGREEMENTS

You may wish to let just part of your home and still "live-in". If you do so you may create an assured tenancy if the guest has exclusive possession of at least part of your home (usually the bedroom), or a licence if all the facilities are shared. The latter agreement is often used for lodgers on a casual basis, but should not be seen as an attempt to avoid giving potential tenants protection. It should be used in genuine sharing situations. In both cases, a tenancy or a licence, your guest is not given protection from eviction if you continue to live-in. The Protection from Eviction Act 1977 only applies to such tenancies and licence arrangements where the landlord does **not** live on the premises. A licence cannot be granted in the case of a self-contained one person flat/bedsit and also if you move away from the property an assured tenancy will again be created giving the tenant security from eviction.

### 6.4  "RENT A ROOM" SCHEME

This was introduced in 1992 to encourage home-owners to let out parts of their homes. Lenders should have no objection to you letting out part of your home to help pay the mortgage - as long as you keep them informed. Also, as part of a government approved scheme, you will not be liable to pay tax provided the income is no more than £3,250 per year. Remember that a tenancy of the room will be created if you grant your guest exclusive possession of that room. You cannot enter than room without the tenant's permission. Purely shared arrangements would be under the auspices of a licence agreement. If you are considering selling your home, the lender will probably ask the tenant to sign a waiver of their rights as a sitting tenant.

If you earn more than £3,250 in rental income per annum you can either stay within the Rent-a-Room scheme or pay tax on the whole amount minus expenses (water rates, ground rents, council tax, normal repairs and redecoration, wear and tear and management expenses). If you stay within the Scheme you will be taxed on your gross income, less £3,250. No further deductions for expenses will be allowed.

### 6.5  COMPANY LETS

If you are moving overseas or to another posting in the UK, you could consider letting your home to a company for the temporary use of its employees, officers or visitors. AST's can only be given to individuals so a separate company let form has to be drafted. But notice still has to be served to bring the tenancy to an end. Again you will need a court order to evict any troublesome tenants. A company letting agreement should only be given to a company which genuinely requires temporary accommodation for its staff etc. If the company concerned has a requirement to house an employee on a more long-term basis, then you ought to consider entering into an AST with the employee direct (provided the agreement is for a period exceeding six months). The company could then act as guarantor for the monthly payments.

## *6.6* OUT OF SEASON LETS

If you have a holiday or second home, you may wish to generate income by letting it out during the out of season months. Again the court must order possession provided the tenancy created is for a term of not more than eight months and at some stage during the twelve months before the out of season tenancy is created, you have let the property out as holiday accommodation to genuine holiday-makers. If you let this property during the holiday season, then the short-term holiday makers acquire no security of tenure and no protection from eviction.

## *6.7* FIRE SAFETY

If you let out your home furnished, the furniture offered must comply with the Furniture and Furnishings (Fire) (Safety) (Amendment) Regulations 1993. The Regulations apply to new and used furniture ordinarily intended for private use in a dwelling and includes, beds, divans, sofa-beds, cushions, mattresses and pillows, but does **not** include bedding or floor coverings. An ignitability test is required of the furniture - the easiest way to tell if your furniture is legal is by looking for a permanent label which will indicate whether the Regulations have been complied with. If not, the penalty could be a very heavy fine. The Regulations do not apply to furniture manufactured before 1st January 1950 nor to material supplied for recovering or reupholstering furniture made before that date.

# Chapter 7

## Dealing with the neighbours

*"Neighbours ... everybody needs good neighbours..."*

Forgive the theft from this infamous antipodean signature tune, but it is true that we all need good neighbours to make urban living tolerable. Unless you are fortunate enough to live in the country with only the trees and the sheep for company, living with neighbours is an integral and important part of home ownership. You may live in a dream home with all the amenities you could need close by, but have a nightmare family living next door. Or squatters, or noisy students or just plain scruffy neighbours. The list goes on. You can always change your home's appearance, but you cannot move its location. If you are contemplating a move try very hard not to get too emotionally involved with potential purchases. You may visit such houses during the daytime or on a quiet Sunday afternoon, quite oblivious to the nocturnal goings-on in the adjoining property. If necessary, make repeated visits to the home at different times of the day to get a feel for the neighbourhood. Speak with local residents - is anyone nearby noted for being particularly troublesome? How are the neighbouring properties kept - neat and tidy with a clear sense of pride or run down and tatty with bags of refuse outside?

Of course this detective work is only good up to a point. You could live in neighbourly bliss for many years only for your neighbours to move out and be replaced with the family from hell. Then life becomes altogether more difficult. The most common areas for conflict between neighbours arise over boundaries, fences and walls, responsibility for water and sewage supplies, noise, trespass, access, light, pets, children, trees and cars and driveways. These will all be dealt with in more detail shortly. Neighbour disputes are certainly not a new phenomenon. Over 70 years ago, G.K. Chesterton wrote,

> *"Your next door neighbour is not a man; he is an environment. He is the barking of a dog; he is the noise of a pianola; he is the dispute about a party wall; he is drains that are worse than yours, or roses that are better than yours."*

## 7.1 BOUNDARIES/FENCES

This is a very rich source of dispute as an Englishman's castle clearly extends to his garden and adjoining property. The problem is most acute with terraced or semi-detached properties where your land abuts your neighbour's. The general rule is that the boundary is marked by the wall or fence which separates the properties and that the person who puts up the fence owns it. If you are unsure about where the fence should go or whether your neighbour has encroached onto your property, the first place to look is the plan attached to the deeds to your property (or the leasehold agreement if not freehold). You can contact your local Land Registry who should supply copies of the relevant plans for a small fee. The plan should indicate with a 'T' where the boundaries lie. But if the deeds make no mention of where the boundary is, there is a presumption which states that it belongs to the land on the side of the vertical support posts. There is generally no legal obligation to erect a fence between yours and your neighbour's property. Where there is a requirement to fence, it will usually be because of a covenant obliging you to do so. If instead there is a hedge and a ditch, a court will assume that the person who dug the ditch did so at the boundary of his land and then planted the hedge on top of the earth from that ditch. The boundary is then assumed to run along the edge of the ditch furthest away from the hedge. But this presumption can be overturned if you can show evidence to the contrary. If there are any long-standing residents who can remember when the ditch was dug and the hedge planted which confirms that the boundary is elsewhere, this will help.

If when you consult the plan it seems that you have more land than originally entitled to i.e. the boundary line is seemingly further on to your neighbour's land than it should be, you can only claim that land as yours if the neighbour has not allowed the encroachment and not qualified it in any way (for example has not given his permission) during the previous twelve years. This is called adverse possession. The twelve year period is cumulative so if you move in after 11 years, you will only have to wait a further twelve months before the land is legally yours. At that point, you may consider seeing a solicitor to have the deeds formally altered. Where a boundary follows a physical feature, certain legal presumptions can be relied upon:

**Footpaths, bridleways and public paths**. A footpath is a highway over which exists a public right of way on foot. A bridleway gives the public a right of way on foot or horseback. A public path can be either.

**Highways**. The boundary of any land adjoining a highway runs down the middle of that highway.

**Rivers**. In respect of non-tidal rivers, the presumption is that the owner of the land which abuts the river owns the bed of the river to the middle of it. For tidal rivers, the bed is the property of the Crown at any point at which the river regularly flows and reflows. The boundary is presumed to be the mean high water mark.

**Seashore**. If you own land which adjoins the sea, then you are presumed to own it up to the mean high-water mark. Reclaimed land always belongs to the Crown.

**Streams**. As with a non-tidal river, the bed will be your responsibility up to the middle of the stream.

If you have a problem over a purported boundary line, always try to talk it through with your neighbour. Land ownership is an incredibly personal issue to many people, so sneaking out under cover of darkness and moving the fence posts is definitely not to be recommended! Get all your evidence together before you make any wild assertions to your neighbour's land. Try to be reasonable and allow him to make his own enquiries. If all this fails, then you may have to resort to legal remedies - perhaps a mandatory injunction forcing the neighbour to move his fence. This is likely to be a very expensive exercise involving solicitors so it is clearly in everybody's interests to reach an amicable solution.

## 7.2  SEWERS AND DRAINS

A public sewer is one built by the Sewerage Undertaker or built by others and is subsequently the responsibility of the Sewerage Undertaker. Also a sewer which drained two or more houses built before 1st October 1937 is termed a public sewer. The responsibility for the maintenance of public sewers rests with your local water company. A private sewer is any sewer built after 1st October 1937 up to the point of intersection with the public sewer. All sink wastes, toilet connections, septic tanks, cesspits and soakaways are private and therefore the responsibility of the property owner (or owners if the sewer is shared).

Figure 1 explains in simple terms neighbours' responsibility for drains and sewers. It is clear that if a private sewer breaks at point 'X' the responsibility for its repair will rest with all the adjoining home owners. But it may well be that one of the houses will suffer the effects much more seriously than the others. It is likely to be this household which effects the repairs. Before doing so you should firstly check to see whether you have any insurance cover (unlikely) and secondly, notify all the affected neighbours and put an estimate of remedial costs to them. Make quite clear at the outset that the responsibility is joint and that everyone will be liable in equal shares (assuming that one of the households has not exacerbated or caused the problem due to negligence - in which case it would be unreasonable to expect everyone to share the costs). Ultimately if you alone are lumbered with the repair bill, you may have to sue to recover your outlay. The contractor who carries out the work will not really care who pays him, but will probably pursue the household which made first contact. In terms of fresh water supplies, the situation is broadly similar. The water company is responsible for the pipes shown as follows:

- the water main in the road.
- the supply pipe from the main to the point where it reaches your boundary.
- the stopcock which marks the above intersection.

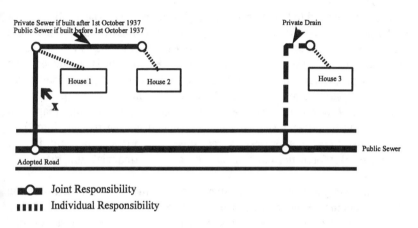

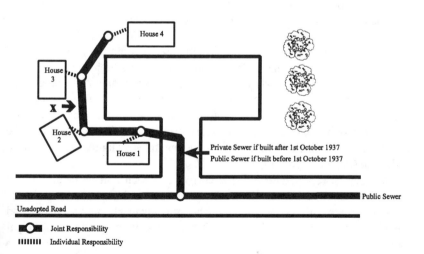

**Figure 1. Neighbours' responsibility for drains and sewers.**

Therefore, any leaks from the stopcock to your home will be your responsibility even if that pipe first passes under your neighbour's land. If you fail to carry out the repairs within a reasonable period, the water company may come along and do so and present you with the bill.

## 7.3 NOISE

If you have ever had to live with noisy neighbours you will know full well just what a problem it is. Victims who put up with noise nuisance may suffer from stress, depression and acute sleep loss. Between 1980 and 1993 domestic noise complaints rose from 31,000 to over 88,000. It is estimated that seventeen people have died recently during arguments caused by loud noise late at night, such as music, car and house burglar alarms and engines being over-revved. Many more have been injured and previously mild-mannered and law-abiding citizens suddenly feel compelled to take the law into their own hands. Local authorities do recognise the problem but are largely powerless to enforce the existing law because of financial and manpower restraints.

Noise is generally quite a subjective problem. Students living in a mansion block of flats may be generally much more tolerant of late-night music than a family living on an estate. The key is really whether the noise is unreasonable. Every case will turn on its own facts - if you live in a modern development of flats you are probably quite tolerant of footsteps above and the odd rattle from the washing machine. If you live in a large, detached home with thick stone walls, you may be much more sensitive to noise from outside. But if the washing machine in the upstairs flat is being used at 4 am three times a week, do you have to put up with such nocturnal disturbances? Probably not.

In the first instance, tackle your neighbour in person on an amicable basis. It is not a good idea to send poisonous notes or make heated telephone calls. If possible ask the neighbour to come into your home whilst his "noise" is in full swing. It may be that he is simply unaware of the problem and needs to be educated. Explain the effect it is having on you and your family. Try to reason with him. Can a compromise be reached?

In many cases, by following the correct approach and by being sure of your facts you will be able to reach a workable solution to the problem. However, there will be neighbours who are downright unreasonable and unwilling to listen. To deal with such problems, there are three principal remedies.

### A civil action for nuisance

Here you would have to issue proceedings through your local county court claiming an injunction to prevent the source of the noise, and damages (financial compensation) for the detrimental effect the noise has had on your life. This can be quite a complicated and expensive process although the remedy ought to be available through the small claims division of your local county court. The main problem will be in convincing the judge that your neighbour's noise is unreasonable. To do so will require much supporting evidence - keep a detailed diary of incidents, get your other neighbours to come along and support, and if you have been to see your GP because of sleeping problems, ask him to write a letter in confirmation. Civil claims for nuisance are relatively uncommon and should be seen as something of a last resort.

## Action through the magistrates' court

If you have a noisy neighbour, consider contacting an Environmental Health Officer (EHO) at the local authority. Again evidence will be the key, but if you can prove a statutory nuisance, defined as, *"noise emitted from premises so as to be prejudicial to health or a nuisance,"* then the EHO can issue a Noise Abatement Notice against the troublesome neighbour. The Notice compels the neighbour not to make the noise complained about. If the Notice is not complied with, the EHO can issue criminal proceedings in the magistrates' court under the Environmental Protection Act 1990 (EPA). The penalty is then a fine of up to £5000 and ultimately a prison term. The magistrates also have the power to seize the source of the noise - such as a hi-fi system. But only about 3% of complaints result in prosecution. Local authorities are responsible for enforcing the Act but have limited resources to do so. Three London boroughs take the problem seriously and have set up specific noise patrol units to investigate complaints. But such action is rare.

If the local authority refuses to issue a Notice Abatement Notice or refuses to prosecute if one is breached, you can complain yourself to the magistrates' court using a summons. If you can produce sound evidence to show that a statutory nuisance has been created, the magistrates can offer you the same enforcement measures as the local authority. There may also be local by-laws open to both you and the local authority to prosecute noisy neighbours. For example a persistently barking dog could have its owners prosecuted provided they have been served with fourteen days' written notice that you regard the noise as a nuisance. The notice must be signed by two other households within hearing distance. If the barking dog continues beyond the fourteenth day his owners can be prosecuted in the magistrates' court.

## Local mediation groups

As with so much of the law today, mediation and arbitration seem to offer an alternative to traditional remedies. The local authorities with the most chronic noise problems (often inner city, high population densities) have realised just how destructive an effect loud music can have. They have also been alive to the fact that many of their residents do not have the funds or the energy to pursue matters through the courts. Instead, small mediation groups such as Mediation UK (see Useful Addresses) have been established which bring the complainant and noise-maker together in an open forum. Skilled counsellors then act as arbitrators in seeking to resolve the problem. Each party is encouraged to see the other's side of the story and to reach a workable solution. The first couple of meetings may prove to be very aggressive with neither party prepared to concede any ground. However in time, tempers may be brought under control and some realism permitted to enter the equation. Contact you local authority to see if it operates such a scheme.

## 7.4 TRESPASS

Trespass is also a familiar problem to many homeowners. In essence it means to "pass beyond", i.e. to go beyond the boundaries of your land without your consent. You could erect a sign along the lines of, *"Keep Out - Trespassers Will Be Shot (or Prosecuted)"*. But in practice, because of the vagaries of the law, it would have no effect. If your neighbour comes on to your land, he will not have committed a **criminal** offence. The remedy lies with the civil law.

If your neighbour is persistently "trespassing" on your property then in the first instance you should try the polite approach. For example, if he leaves his mower on your rear patio on an habitual basis, ask him to desist. If the problem is not immediately remedied or if you suffer from people trampling over your prize begonias, you could sue and seek an injunction to prevent a repetition, together with financial compensation for the damage caused. As with an injunction for noise, you must be sure of your evidence - keep a diary, take photos or a video. Do you have other neighbours who are prepared to support you contentions? Financial compensation will only be awarded in the more extreme cases - in most, if people have merely been on your land, then proving an actual loss which is more than de minimis could be problematic. In any event such proceedings will be costly and most homeowners will not qualify for Legal Aid without at least some contribution towards legal costs. You could try self-help remedies by making a trespass on your property more difficult. Refencing or prickly bushes etc. may all help. But you could easily overstep the mark so it would be advisable to stop short of putting mines in the vegetable patch and electrifying the larch-lap fencing!

## 7.5 LIGHT

No one has a God-given right to light. Acquiring such a right may be possible through prescription (see Chapter 1). If you do have such a right, then the question which may arise from neighbouring structures is not how much light has been lost, but how much remains? Infringing your right to light can only be done by a man-made structure - if the neighbour erects a twelve foot satellite dish, then a court would be asked to consider the locality and type of room affected and the hours of sunlight it normally received. You are much more likely to succeed in a claim for damages if your living room is cast into shadow than a functional utility room. Again, establishing a legal case may not be too difficult but having the resources and evidence to take it to court may be beyond many homeowners.

## 7.6 VIEWS

You can never acquire a right to a view, even if the value of your home is greatly diminished by an eyesore.

## 7.7 PETS

If your neighbour's dog comes onto your property and eats all your prize leeks or kills your Koi Carp, he may well be financially liable to you provided the neighbour has been negligent. In one case you will not even have to prove negligence - if the owner has reason to believe that his otherwise harmless pooch has a tendency to "turn", then liability is strict - you need not prove negligence. You cannot force your neighbours to contain their pets by erecting a fence. Persistent straying onto your land *could* give rise to a nuisance claim. If you are injured or the animal damages your property then you are entitled to compensation under the Animals Act 1971 provided you can show that the neighbour failed to take reasonable steps to restrain the animal or actively encouraged it to cause the damage.

The Dangerous Dogs Act 1991 was introduced to deal with dogs such as American pit bull terriers. If such a dog is *dangerously* out of control in a public place, then the owner can be prosecuted through the criminal courts. If convicted, he could be heavily fined or even sent to prison. If you suspect that your neighbour is being cruel or has abandoned his pet, contact your local RSPCA - prosecutions (though rare) can be brought, but more importantly, the animal can be taken into safe custody. Noisy dogs and fouling the footpath are dealt with by local by-laws. Contact your Environmental Health Officer for assistance.

## 7.8 TREES

A tree will remain the property of the landowner by whom it was planted - even when its trunk, roots and branches extend to adjoining property. The encroachment of branches or tree roots is a nuisance. It may also give rise to a statutory liability and rights of abatement by local authorities (i.e. your council could issue an abatement notice forcing the tree owner to take certain action). You can only sue your neighbour for nuisance if you have suffered damage from the offending root or branch. In terms of roots the damage may be obvious, for example a broken or blocked drain etc. However simple abstraction of water from the soil may well suffice as it is likely to make the area unstable and could lead to subsidence, particularly if the soil has a high clay content. If your foundations or drains etc. are damaged by your neighbour's tree roots, then you will have to involve your insurers.

In turn your insurance company may pursue your neighbour (or his insurers) and make recommendations to remove the tree. In terms of self-help remedies you are legally entitled to remove roots which encroach on to your land. This applies also to offending branches which overhang your airspace. But remember that the branches remain the property of your neighbour so you should check with him that it is acceptable for you to dispose of them. Also, before you get chain saw happy, you should check with the local authority that the tree in question is not the subject of a Tree Preservation Order (TPO) (see Chapter 4.)

Damage caused by falling tree branches is a common problem and often a rich source of dispute between neighbours. But your neighbour will only be liable for damage caused to your property if you can prove negligence. For example, if your neighbour has a badly rotting tree in his garden which has been breaking down over the past couple of winters, and a branch falls off and smashes your greenhouse, you will have a valid claim. If it were a healthy tree and the winds were exceptional, then clearly the landowner would not have been negligent.

## 7.9 CHILDREN

There is probably no denying that at times, children can be a real nuisance! For most homeowners the problems are relatively transient and not too severe. From crying through the night during the early stages to loud parties during the late teenage years. Stray footballs through the greenhouse or onto the cabbage patch should also be expected. So living next to a family with children demands a certain degree of tolerance. Friction is most likely to occur when a retired couple live next door to a young family with three boisterous sons. Simply, the older couple has forgotten what it takes to run a family whilst the young family regard their neighbours as interfering old busy bodies. But the problems can become more severe and stretch tolerance levels to the maximum. A child that persistently comes on to your land and damages your property, in theory, can be sued just like his parent. But the age of the child will be of significance in determining whether he knew or ought to have known that his actions were wrong. A four year old who throws a stone at your window probably would not be liable. An eleven year old almost certainly would be. But in any event these arguments are rather academic as the child will not be worth suing - unless you know that they have money of their own. Similarly the child's parents cannot be held *financially* liable for the proven wrongdoing of their children.

The parent may be worth suing in their own right. To do so you would have to show either that the parent had failed to exercise proper control over the child and that the resulting damage was reasonably foreseeable or that the parent had encouraged the child to act in a certain way. Again age will be an important consideration. It would be difficult to hold a parent liable for the negligent act of a sixteen year old boy and his bicycle. But if a seven year old runs amok in your garden on an habitual basis and the parent fails to heed the warnings, he may well be liable to you. It is also worth bearing in mind that as a homeowner you must take extra care if there are children about. A compost heap at the bottom of your open garden may pose no particular threat to adults. But if it has a ramp up to it or an attractive series of steps, it may prove to be too much of a temptation for playing children. If you have failed to take account of this risk and damage or injury results, you will be liable in negligence.

## 7.10 ACCESS
Homeowners can become very possessive about their land and refuse access for even things such as pruning trees or painting the overhanging eaves. Technically you need your neighbour's permission to enter his land to carry out repairs etc. To do so without his consent would amount to a civil trespass. But as already discussed, the practical remedies open to your neighbour means that any legal action is unlikely unless you have to erect semi-permanent scaffolding etc. If permission is not granted, then you can apply to your local county court for an order giving access to do the work. Such an application is made under the Access To Neighbouring Land Act 1992. You must include the following:

• details of the land and why access is necessary.
• evidence to show why you will have to go onto the neighbouring land.
• some form of undertaking to make good any damage.
• a time estimate for the work.

## 7.11 RUBBISH/SMELLS
For the most part you will have to tolerate untidy and/or smelly neighbours. Simply, you cannot force people to be tidy. Overpowering smells could amount to a nuisance actionable through the courts. But it would have to be a persistent problem of which you have detailed evidence in support. Obviously

you cannot capture a smell on film so contact your neighbours and seek their support. A call to the local EHO should also be considered. In terms of untidy neighbours, there may be some redress under planning or local by-laws. If the mess is highly visible and spoiling the local neighbourhood's amenity, contact your local authority. It can serve a notice on your neighbour compelling him to take action. In extreme cases it can even remove the rubbish itself and hold the neighbour liable for the costs. Every case will turn on its own facts. If you live in a quiet wholly residential street where there is a strong sense of community pride, then the chances of succeeding against a sole offensive neighbour will be much greater than if you live in a run-down urban area.

### 7.12  PARKING/COMMERCIAL USE OF A RESIDENTIAL HOME
These may amount to breaches of planning law (See Chapter 4 for details).

### 7.13  CAR/HOUSE BURGLAR ALARMS
Whilst house and car alarms are a reaction to the tidal wave of property crime, a false alarm can be an incredible nuisance. If you live in an urban area you may have become almost immune to the problem and the deterrent effect may be brought into question. But for many, alarms from neighbouring homes or cars are a nuisance. The good news is that legislation has been introduced to keep pace with the problem. Also, under a Code of Practice for manufacturers, all new burglar alarms since 1st April 1992 have to cut out after twenty minutes. If the alarm rings for more than sixty minutes an EHO can apply to a Justice of the Peace (JP) for a warrant. Armed with this the EHO can effectively self-abate the noise by attending the property and doing what is necessary to shut off the power. The EHO has to leave the property in a secure state. Neighbours and local authorities alike also have the power to apply for an abatement notice under S.79 of the Environmental Protection Act 1990 (see previously). The Noise and Statutory Nuisances Act 1993 now covers noise from vehicles - including alarms. Again you should contact the EHO if a nearby car is particularly troublesome - he will then try for one hour to ascertain who is the owner of the vehicle. If this fails to produce a satisfactory silence, then the EHO can, under the supervision of a police officer disable the car alarm. This will usually entail calling out a locksmith although any associated costs will usually have to be borne by the car's owner.

### 7.14  FALLING ROOF TILES
Surprisingly, if a roof tile blows off your property and damages your neighbour's home or car, insurance is unlikely to cover the remedial costs. It is regarded as an Act of God. However, you could be personally liable in negligence if you knew of the risk but had failed to take preventive action.

# Chapter 8

## Dealing with tradesmen/consumer law generally

Buying the shell of a house is only the start of things to come. It has to be furnished, decorated, perhaps extended, cleaned and maintained. To fulfil some or even all of these requirements will require assistance from professionals whose various services effectively have to be bought into. This opens up a whole new area of law and dealing effectively as a consumer is an important part of homeownership. We are consumers of goods - perhaps a new pair of curtains or a satellite TV, and consumers of services - the seamstress who made the curtains or the satellite TV installer.

This chapter aims to explain the law relevant to consumers and to discuss effective complaint/enforcement tactics. The final section deals in particular with proceedings through the small claims division of the county court. Although intended to be user-friendly and to avoid the need for lawyers, the prospect of any court action is daunting for many. A real-life example is shown to unravel at least some of the mystery. Many tradesmen, retailers and professionals are members of governing bodies. Some offer very little by way of protection to the consumer. Many however do operate a viable alternative to court proceedings under an arbitration procedure (See Useful Addresses for further details).

## 8.1 CONSUMER LAW GENERALLY

Confusion still reigns for consumers. Whilst the principal piece of legislation, the Sale of Goods Act has been around since 1893, many people are still unsure of their rights. The retailers have contributed in no small part to this confusion by offering their own customer policies. Where one high street store may be quite happy to refund or replace goods for whatever reason, another may apply the law strictly and seemingly offer no service to its customers. So if you buy a pair of socks from Marks & Spencer and subsequently decide that you do not like the colour, they will happily offer a refund on production of a valid receipt. But if you buy the latest state-of-the-art power drill for your current DIY project and subsequently decide that you do not like the colour, do not be surprised if the likes of B&Q say that they cannot help - even if the drill is unused, still in the box and you have a receipt.

The law is actually quite clear - if a product is **defective** and you reject it within a reasonable period, you are entitled to your money back or a replacement - the choice is yours. If you simply don't like the item, for example it is the wrong colour, the retailer is under no obligation to refund replace or offer a credit note. Many retailers will however - this is purely in addition and in excess of your statutory rights. If you buy items in a sale or shop soiled, your rights are exactly the same. Some shops may put up a notice to the effect that sale goods are 'sold as seen' and replacements/refunds will not be considered in any circumstances. This is illegal. The Sale of Goods Ac

1979 as amended by the Sale and Supply of Goods Act 1994 is now the principal governing legislation. The law requires that goods sold by retailers in the course of their business:

## Fit their description

The make and specification etc. The key to a possible failure to sell an item as described is whether you get what you bargained for. This is very much dependent upon the facts of each case, but if you have been sold for example, "the 1996 Deluxe hammer drill" from Dlack & Becker, which is clearly not, then you will have a remedy; rejection or damages. In most cases some form of compensation ought to be attainable - if you've got a better deal than you thought, keep quiet, otherwise ascertain what the retailer is prepared to offer.

## Be of satisfactory quality

This new term should widen the scope for effective complaint to disappointed consumers. Under the old requirement - merchantable quality - judges and lawyers alike had difficulty in agreeing on a satisfactory definition. Consumers were just supposed to know instinctively whether their purchases were of merchantable quality. Of great significance now is the need for goods to be free of minor defects. But such defects will only give you cause to complain provided they were not brought properly to your attention before you bought. Satisfactory quality is dependent to a degree on the market at which the product is aimed.

## Be fit for their purpose

This condition was often used as an alternative to a claim being made for goods which were not of merchantable quality. Any item, new or used ought to be fit for the purpose for which it is reasonably used. Any claims of unfitness for purpose will really only arise where you have made specific requirements of the retailer. For example if you requested that your new carpet be stain resistant and it was sold on this basis, then a claim for damages will lie if the first upset cup of tea, leaves an indelible stain. Every case will necessarily turn on its own facts.

If when you buy an item as a consumer it falls down on one or all of these points, you must consider taking it back and insisting on a full refund. As soon as you realise that you have a problem, contact the retailer concerned. Ideally speak with someone in a position of authority and clearly point out the problem. Be firm and state that you wish to return the item and claim additional financial compensation for out of pocket expenses (if appropriate). The law states that you have a *reasonable* period for rejection. It is difficult to quantify what is meant by this although the cases have shown that the period is much shorter than many people may think. In the past the right to reject was lost if you indicated an acceptance of the item and its problems. Under the new law, you will not be in danger of being treated as having accepted the item simply by requesting or agreeing to a repair. Also you must be allowed a reasonable opportunity to find out whether the product does conform to the legal requirements before you can be deemed to have accepted it. If you are outside the reasonable period for rejection or if you have been deemed to have accepted, your remedy will be to claim damages - financial compensation.

Some retailers are very receptive to genuine complaints about their products. Many however are unlikely to accept your protestations and offer a refund. So it is important that you are firm and sure of your evidence. Be prepared to confirm everything in writing and to keep notes of all associated expenses. If you have been misled by advertising literature or if the product associated is dangerous, contact your local Trading Standards Officer (TSO), who may wish to consider the merits of pursuing a criminal action. Be reasonable in your expectations - has the product complained of really only been the subject of *fair* wear and tear or has it been hacked to pieces?

### Checklist
- you will need a receipt or other proof of purchase.
- if you are rejecting a product, do so as soon as possible.
- complain in writing.
- keep your cool!
- keep copies of all supporting evidence.
- try not to be sidetracked - stick to your guns.
- be prepared to think laterally - are dispute resolution options open?
- be reasonable in your expectations.
- be prepared to seek an expert's opinion to confirm the defect.
- never complain solely on a point of principle *and* expect to win!

### 8.2 THE CONSUMER PROTECTION ACT 1987 (CPA)

Though surprisingly little used, the CPA can be a very useful weapon in the consumer's armoury. The basic principle of the CPA is that producers are liable for damage caused by their products. Importantly for consumers, you do not need to establish any fault and there need not be any contractual relationship between you and the producer (i.e. you need not have bought the item). A form of strict liability is thereby created.

The burden of proof is still on the consumer to show the damage, the defect and the link between them, but you need not prove negligence (previously a major stumbling block). Of course as consumers a right always exists against the seller - the other contracting party. This is an important aspect of consumer law so do not be fobbed off by a retailer who tells you to take up your problem with the manufacturer. But under the CPA if you have bought a defective product which causes damage (injury, death or damage to private property) and the value of your claim is at least £275, you have an equal right to hold the producer liable. This may be important if the seller is less than financially secure.

Anyone wishing to claim under the CPA must commence proceedings within ten years of the product being supplied. A further limitation is that you must issue proceedings within three years of becoming aware of the damage, the defect and the identity of the supplier/producer, subject to the ultimate cut-off at ten years. So if you are injured five years after the product was supplied you have until year eight. Of course many products are not expected to last ten years. The definition of defect takes account of perishable and consumable items and others suffering wear and tear as part of what consumers are generally entitled to expect. Provided the producer gives instruction, if appropriate, on the need to use within a period, servicing intervals and replacement of parts etc., he will not be liable.

## 8.3 BUYING WITH CREDIT

The introduction of hire purchase (HP) in the 1960's revolutionised the way consumers were able to equip and furnish their homes. It coincided with technological advancements so that for the first time automatic washing machines and colour televisions became available to the masses. Buying with credit is now more popular than ever and the types of finance on offer can be considerably more sophisticated than our old friend the HP agreement. As consumers your rights vary according to the type of agreement, but the main piece of legislation is the Consumer Credit Act 1974 (CCA).

### Hire purchase

Under an HP agreement you do not own the item concerned - the monthly payment is simply in return for the finance company hiring the item to you. You therefore have no rights over the hired item in respect of resale or otherwise disposing of it. At the end of the hire period the finance company will transfer the ownership of the item to you on receipt of a further nominal sum. You can then sell it on to a third party without fear of reprisal. When you buy on HP you will normally be asked to fill out a credit proposal form at the retailer concerned's premises. Provided your application is successful, then the retailer will "sell" you the item and be reimbursed in due course by the finance company concerned (who will effectively own the item).

## Cooling off

What if you realise that you cannot afford the payments? There is no blanket right to cancel but it may exist if the agreement was signed off trade premises (perhaps in your home). If you signed at the premises of the retailer at the same time as the trader - you cannot cancel. If you concluded the agreement at home you have a five day cooling-off period. This period starts to run once you have received through the post the second copy of the agreement which spells out your cancellation rights. To cancel effectively you must do so in writing. The effect is to bring the whole agreement to an end. You should be refunded any sums which you paid in advance. If the finance company fails to serve the agreements at the correct stage or if notices etc. are lacking then the agreement is unenforceable. You may wish to see a solicitor if you think that you have been given a defective agreement.

## Repossession

You must keep up the payments. If you do get into difficulty, contact the finance company concerned. It may reschedule the payments or waive the interest for a few months to help you get out of a hole. Before the finance company can take any action, it must serve a default notice which states the nature of the breach and what must be done to remedy it. If you have made more than one third of the payments, then the finance company cannot repossess the item from you without a court order. Otherwise it may instruct bailiffs to repossess - but this does **not** mean that they can come into your home unless invited to do so. Do not be misled by what you may have seen on TV - bailiffs smashing in external doors and windows without a court order is **illegal**.

## Early payment

If the HP agreement is for £15,000 or less, then the CCA gives you the right to settle early and obtain a rebate on the interest charges to reflect the early payment. But repaying early may provide a few shocks as the sum quoted (the settlement figure) may be higher than expected to accommodate the lost interest of the finance company. To find out this figure, which is calculated according to the CCA, contact the company concerned in writing. They are obliged to give you the information, but you are not then obliged to settle early.

## Rejecting goods

In many respects buying on finance is good news for the consumer as your rights will remain in the force against the finance company throughout the duration of the agreement (which may be several years). Also the Supply o

Goods (Implied Terms) Act 1973 imports the same requirements of goods bought with cash, viz. fitness for purpose, satisfactory quality, as described etc., into goods "bought" under a finance agreement. To reject the item, tell the finance company that the goods are not of satisfactory quality, that you are rejecting them, and that they are available to be collected. If you can satisfy the finance company that the item is not of the required legal standard, then you should have any instalments already paid, refunded.

### Bank/building society loans
If you take out a simple loan to fund a consumer purchase, you are effectively paying with cash as far as the retailer is concerned and afforded no special protection.

### Credit cards
Buying with a credit card can give you extra protection by virtue of S.75 of the CCA 1974. Under this section, provided the value of the goods bought is more than £150, then the card issuer as well as the retailer is liable to you for any problems. The credit card company is therefore said to be jointly and severally liable. This protection may be particularly useful if the retailer becomes insolvent. If the problem is about the quality of an item purchased (i.e. the retailer is in breach of contract) complain in writing in the usual way. If this fails to prompt a result, copy all the correspondence in to the credit card company holding it liable under S.75. Be perserverant. The card company will probably deny that they are liable. This is wrong so if you have a problem, contact the Office of Fair Trading (OFT, see Useful Addresses). Note that S.75 protection only applies to **credit** cards; not debit or charge cards such as American Express.

## 8.4 CREDIT REFERENCE AGENCIES
Before you are granted any type of credit, the finance company must satisfy itself that you are a good credit risk - i.e. that you can make the repayments. To check on your rating the finance company will conduct a search with one of the major credit reference agencies. If you are turned down you should ask which agency was approached. Contact them in writing enclosing £1 and ask for a copy of your credit file. If the file contains incorrect information then you have the right, in up to two hundred words, to place a notice of correction on file. The agency must place the correction on your file and may send a copy of it to anyone who has consulted it during the previous six months. If you still have problems in obtaining credit (unjustifiably), then complain to the OFT.

## 8.5 UNSOLICITED GOODS

These are goods which are sent to you without being requested. They are usually accompanied by a demand for money. Fortunately the practice is not as common as it used to be and was actually outlawed by the Unsolicited Goods and Services Act 1971. Now if you do receive unsolicited goods you are at liberty to treat them as if they had been given as an unconditional gift provided:

- you have done nothing with the goods for the first six months or,
- you give written notice to the sender that he should collect the goods within the preceding thirty days.

## 8.6 DEALING WITH TRADESMEN

Tradesmen - plumbers, carpenters, electricians etc., tend to fall into two very broad categories. They are either tagged as stetson-wearing cowboys or craftsmen who carry out the work for the sake of a dying art! Of course this sort of generalisation is grossly unfair but perpetuated largely by us all as consumers of their services. We seldom talk of satisfactory jobs - only the extremes seem worthy of gossip. But satisfactory or even good workmanship is quite clearly the norm.

The Supply of Goods and Services Act 1982 requires that the work done is to a reasonable standard using suitable materials of satisfactory quality. Reasonable standard does not mean an exceptional level of skill - it means the standard which could be expected of a reasonably competent member of the particular trade or profession. It may be that you approach an architect to draw up some plans and thereafter to oversee the building of an extension. If he arranges for the building services and the supply of materials, then you will effectively have one contract enforceable against the architect (assuming that you pay only the architect). If there are problems then he may well say that you should seek a resolution with the builder directly. This is wrong. In most cases however the contractual situation will be much simpler. For example if you buy a carpet from a retailer on a supply only basis and arrange with someone else to have it fitted, you will effectively have two contracts. If the carpet is defective (for example it shades badly) then your gripe is with the retailer (**not** the manufacturer). But if the carpet is fitted poorly or the join stitched badly, then your complaint is with the fitter.

### Complaining

Always contact the tradesman concerned as soon as the problem first comes to light. In most cases a repair will be effected immediately. If the response is less than startling, confirm your complaint in writing. Put a deadline on the issue, perhaps seven or fourteen days. If this still fails to prompt a response, be prepared to seek evidence in support of your contentions. Many tradesmen are only small businesses who may not have the financial backing to entertain your claim - unless pushed. Try and get an expert's report (see Useful Addresses). You will probably have to pay for such a report at the outset, but if favourable to your cause, you will be able to claim the fee on top. Keep details of all your out of pocket expenses - these too should be recoverable. If time is important you must make it clear before the work starts. Make time of the essence. To avoid confusion about the cost, insist on a written **quotation** before the contract is concluded. An oral estimate will be nigh on impossible to enforce.

## Checklist

- always seek out a reputable trader - word of mouth recommendations from friends are the best, not the first name in the phone book.
- check his insurance cover.
- look for a trader who is a member of a professional governing body.
- always insist on a written quotation.
- keep evidence of the problem - photos, video, a diary etc. Can you ask a neighbour to witness?
- consider an expert's report to support your contentions.
- always confirm your complaint in writing.
- be reasonable in your expectations.
- never fight solely on a point of principle *and* expect to win.

If you are sure of your case and you have good evidence in support, you will effectively have two options. Firstly, to sue the trader concerned seeking damages for breach of contract and/or negligence. Or secondly you could instruct another trader to come in and put right the work and then seek recompense. A further alternative could be to invoke the arbitration procedure of the trader's governing body (if it has one). The Glass and Glazing Federation for example offers consumers a very effective complaints procedure against its members who supply and fit double glazing.

## Missed appointments

This is a common and very irksome problem for homeowners. For example your cooker breaks down, so you arrange for a repairer to call sometime on Friday the 13th. When he fails to show you still have not only no cooker, but lost earnings. Can you claim? In practice probably not. Many service companies do now offer customer guarantees and some form of compensation for missed appointments. However if this is not the case then you would have to rely on a verbal appointment and prove your losses. Rather than sue for these, a better approach may be to negotiate a reduction in the final fee charged by the contractor.

## 8.7 UNFAIR CONTRACT TERMS

The Unfair Contract Terms Act 1977 requires that exclusion clauses in consumer contracts satisfy a test of reasonableness. This means that if a retailer or service provider tries to rely on a clause which limits or excludes liability, it must be reasonable. Now, the Unfair Terms in Consumer Contracts Regulations 1994 require that the terms of the contract themselves must be fair. An unfair term will not be binding in a contract for goods and services between a seller or supplier acting in the course of his business and a consumer. Unfair means, *"any term which contrary to the requirement of good faith causes a significant imbalance in the parties' rights and obligations under the contract to the detriment of the consumer."* But interestingly, no assessment of fairness is required of the contract's core provisions, i.e. those which define the main subject matter of the contract.

## 8.8 LITIGATION

If your own attempts at mediation fail or if arbitration is not an option then the only course of action may be to sue. Even the threat of litigation may prompt some action and force a reluctant settlement. Over 90% of civil cases settle before they reach a hearing so do not be put off unduly by the prospect of having to appear in court. For claims of under £3000 you need not use a solicitor. Indeed the small claims procedure was introduced for litigants in person so that no solicitors' fees are allowed - even by the winner. If you choose to instruct a lawyer because you feel unsure, then be prepared to pay all of his fees. An expert's fee however ought to be recoverable from the loser.

### The threatening letter

Before you sue, you should send the other party a letter formally spelling out the problem, what needs to be done to remedy it and the action you will take if not complied with by a set date. Use this opportunity wisely. A well drafted and reasonable letter could save you time and trouble in the long-term. Here are two examples:

## (i)  Worn furniture

*Dear Managing Director*

### Re:  Roller-Luxury 3 Piece Suite £995, purchased November 1995

As you are by now doubtless aware from my previous correspondence with your company (see copies), the above furniture is not of satisfactory quality. I have tried on three occasions to reject the furniture and claim a refund. As this has not been forthcoming I have now obtained an expert's report from the Quality Furnishers' Association. The cost of this report was £75 + VAT.

In view of this expert opinion, perhaps you will reconsider your position and refund the £995 together with the fee for the report. If I do not hear from you positively within the next seven days, I shall be issuing proceedings out of the Brentford County Court, claiming damages, legal costs and interest. I do hope that this matter can be resolved to our mutual satisfaction.

*Yours faithfully*

*ENCS.*

## (ii)  Poor workmanship

*Dear Mr Leakey*

### Re: Defective shower

As you will recall from our earlier telephone conversation, the repair which you attempted to our shower has failed for the second time. On this occasion the carpet was completely flooded. I enclose an estimate for a suitable replacement carpet together with the invoice of Pro Plumbers whom we had to call in to effect emergency repairs.

I would be grateful if you could settle these sums by return. I have been advised by my solicitor that if payment is not forthcoming within the next seven days that I have good grounds to issue court proceedings, the cost of which plus other losses I will seek from you. I look forward to hearing from you.

*Yours sincerely*

*ENCS.*

## Settlement before litigation

The other side may either admit the problem or simply take a view that the commercial reality of the situation demands a settlement of your claim. It may enter into "Without Prejudice" correspondence in an attempt to reach an offer which is acceptable to you. Although misunderstood and often used in the wrong context, any correspondence which is marked "Without Prejudice" cannot subsequently be used in evidence in court proceedings. Such offers are usually made without admission of liability. Here is an example:

### WITHOUT PREJUDICE

*Dear Mr Litigator*

### Re: Roller-Luxury 3 Piece Suite

*I am in receipt of your letter of January 2. I was very sorry to learn of the problems which you have had with the above furniture. This has been a very successful line with no complaints so far. Our technical people do not agree with the statements made by your expert, but as a gesture of goodwill and without admission of liability we are prepared to offer a sum of £500 in full and final settlement of all claims.*

*If this is agreeable, could you please sign the attached form and I will arrange for a cheque to be drawn in your favour. I look forward to hearing from you.*

*Yours sincerely*

If you are faced with such an offer to settle, try not to cave in at the first smell of ready cash. If your case is sound, well-structured and evidenced then there is no reason why you should not pursue the other side for more. But if your case is rather frail or if you simply do not have the energy to continue further, accept the offer and retire gracefully.

## Small claims proceedings

Litigation should be seen as a last resort. A small claim is currently one whose value is less than £3000 and which is dealt with under the arbitration procedure of the county court. There is no "Small Claims Court" as such - merely a way of dealing with a certain type of case. In particular the procedure may be suitable for:

- debt recovery.
- claims against retailers.
- poor workmanship.
- arrears of rent.
- small personal injury or vehicle damage claims.
- claims for nuisance - e.g. against your neighbour.
- defective services.

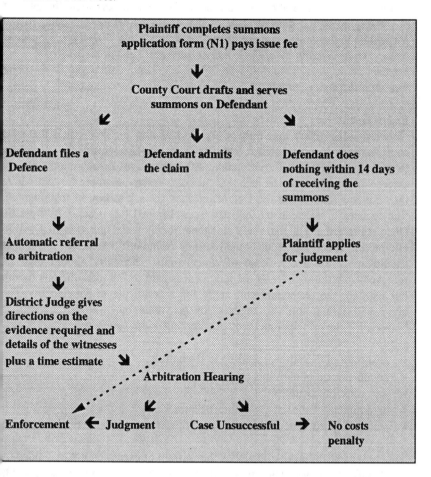

**Table 4. Small claims procedure.**

*Plaintiff* - *person making the assertions, the one who has a claim.*
*Defendant* - *the person against whom the assertions are made.*

This is really only an outline of the procedure. The staff at your local county court can provide you with a series of free leaflets which explain matters in more detail. Local Citizens' Advice Bureaux may also prove to be of assistance (if you can get an appointment!).

## Interest

You can also make a claim for interest up to the date of judgment. You must include the claim for interest in your claim. You should calculate the amount of interest up to the date of issue of the summons before you hand in the particulars to the court. A claim should be worded thus, *"The Plaintiff claims interest under Section 69 of the County Courts Act 1984 at the rate of_____ per cent per annum at the daily rate of £_____ and continuing at the same rate until the date of judgment."*

## Enforcement

Obtaining a judgment may only be the start of your problems. It is merely a court stamped document that A owes B, C pounds. The court itself will not try to get the money out of the defendant. All county court money judgments are entered on a register on the date that the court enters judgment (except where the case is defended and the Defendant does not ask to pay in instalments). The register is overseen by Registry Trust Limited (see Useful Addresses). Once registered, a judgment will stay there for six years unless settled within one month. If the judgment is paid within the month period, the Defendant should apply for a certificate of cancellation. The entry should then be removed from the register. If the judgment is paid in full after the one month has expired, the Defendant can apply for a certificate of satisfaction. The entry will remain on the register for six years but will be marked as "satisfied". The principal methods of enforcing a judgment are:

- a warrant of execution - sending in the bailiffs.
- an attachment of earnings order.
- garnishee proceedings.
- bankruptcy - if the debt is for more than £750.
- a charging order on the home.

The most used and most effective is the warrant of execution but be guided by court staff on the associated procedures and costs. Do not pursue Defendants who have no money - getting the judgment is the easy bit - if a District Judge orders repayment at £5 per month, the victory may prove to be rather hollow in the long-term.

## Paperwork

A completed Form N1 follows. If the particulars of your claim are more detailed and you need more space, it is quite normal to provide these on a separate sheet, headed Particulars of Claim (see Appendix 1).

---

**County Court Summons**          *Case*                  *Always*
                                  *Number*                *quote*
                                                          *this*

                                  *In the*

**(1)**
Plaintiff's
full name          A V Litigator
address            The Penthouse          Justice          County Court
                   22 Acacia Mews
                   London SW99

                   *The court office is open from 10 am to 4 pm Monday to Friday*

**(2)**
Address for
service (and)
payment.
*(if not as above)*                        *Telephone*:
Ref/Tel no.

**(3)**
Defendant's
name               R D Leakey             **Seal**
address.           207 Pipe-Bore Road     *This summons is only valid if*
                   Wellington, Surrey     *sealed by the court. If it is not*
                                          *sealed it should be sent to the*
                                          *court.*

### What the plaintiff claims from you

*Brief*
*description*
*of type of claim*   **Defective Workmanship**

Particulars of the Plaintiff's
claim against you                **Amount claimed**          £450.00

The Defendant failed on two      **Court fee**               £45.00
occasions in December 1995 to
fix the Plaintiff's shower. On   **Solicitor's costs**
the second occasion the work
was of such a poor standard      **Total amount**            £495.00
that a pipe burst and caused
a flood to the Plaintiff's       Summons issued on    26 October 1995
bathroom. A new carpet (£170)
and emergency plumber's fees
(£280) are sought as damages.

---

---

## What to do about this summons

**You can:**
- dispute the claim
- make a claim against the Plaintiff
- admit the claim in full and offer to pay
- pay the total amount shown above
- admit only part of the claim

**Signed**

*For information on what to do or if you need further advice, please turn over.*

**Plaintiff ('s solicitor)**

(or see enclosed particulars of claim)

*Keep this summons, you may need to refer to it.*

*N1 Default Summons (fixed amount) (Order 3, rule 3(2)(b))*

---

## Lay representatives

Appearing in any kind of court hearing can be a daunting prospect. Under the small claims procedure, professional advocates are not encouraged to appear on behalf of their clients. The current no-costs rule makes the whole process uneconomic. You can however instruct a lay representative, perhaps a friend, to represent you at court. Until fairly recently lay representatives had no statutory right to appear - they needed the permission of the District Judge. Now they have a right of audience which means the right to exercise any of the functions of appearing before or addressing a court, including the calling and examining of witnesses. Lay representatives cannot conduct the litigation itself - this includes the issue of proceedings on behalf of the plaintiff. It is also worth noting that the right of audience does not extend to appeals, applications to set aside a judgment or stages after the award has been entered. Any fees of the lay representative will be the personal responsibility of the parties to the litigation.

# Chapter 9

## Home security

The property crime figures in the UK make for very depressing reading. In 1994 alone, there were almost 5 million notifiable offences. Although the number of burglaries is down, to 1.3 million, most homeowners live in fear of the burglar. Burglary accounts for 24% of all crime, so although any improvement in the statistics is to be welcomed, there is still a long, long way to go. A particularly worrying aspect of property crime is the very low clear up rate by the police. This has several knock-on effects - very little property is recovered so homeowners may be forced to claim on their insurance policies. In turn insurers soon get a feel for the highest risk areas which can make obtaining insurance a difficult and very expensive process. Because of the high cost of insurance it is estimated that up to 25% of all households do not have any cover. So if you are burgled or have a fire or suffer some other accidental damage, the cost of replacement and/or repair will be borne by you. A very unsatisfactory situation for any homeowner to be in.

Low clear-up rates also mean little confidence in the police and a real fear that not only are the criminals "getting away with it", but also that they may strike again. In fact statistics tend to support such a fear, and in some areas the risk of being burgled several times is astonishingly high. Perhaps it is no surprise that some people have taken the law into their own hands. The public perception of a police disinterest in property is borne out when clear-up rates for offences such as rape and murder are viewed in comparison. For violent crimes the clear up rate in 1994 was nearly 70%. For murder this figure rises to almost 90%. Obviously reassuring for your family if you meet an untimely death but not much use to you. But if your pedal cycle is stolen there is a 91% chance that you will not see it again. The comparison is probably an unfair reflection on the police and used here as an extreme, but in spite of attempts to identify bikes etc., it seems that such valuable items make for rich and easy pickings amongst the criminal fraternity.

For the homeowner it is not just the burglar to be wary of. In 1994 there were just under one million criminal damage offences reported. Many of these were committed by aggrieved neighbours or errant youths running amok. A brick through your greenhouse or a bent car radio aerial may not sound like the crimes of the century, but for the victims they can be costly, troublesome and uninsured. If the perpetrators are found (clear up rate around 17%) and prosecuted, the convicting court can make a compensation order in your favour. This is usually to the value of the damaged item and, in the case of a broken window etc., the refitting costs. But such orders are only as good as the convicted person. If he has no money or no desire to pay it, you may never be fully compensated or if you are, it may take several years at a nominal monthly repayment rate. Again the honest citizen loses out.

Probably the most distressing aspect of a dwelling-house burglary is the fact that strangers have come in to your home uninvited and perhaps damaged and destroyed personal but valueless items. But this type of burglary is the most risky for the villain. Alarms, dogs and unexpected residents mean that opportunist criminals (the most common type) are far more likely to be caught in the act. Far less risky is theft from allotments and gardens. Who would think that either offered much to the criminal? In fact, there may be some very valuable, highly saleable and difficult to trace items:

- mowers.
- garden tools.
- clothes.
- ornamental pottery.
- planters.
- trees and shrubs.
- bicycles.
- power tools.
- camping equipment.

All of these items plus many more, make easy targets for thieves. Even allotments are regularly targeted. Everything from runner bean canes to cabbages are stolen. Police believe that most of the stolen booty ends up in car boot sales where no questions are ever asked.

## 9.1 SELF-DEFENCE

If you are confronted by a criminal the police usually advise to leave well alone, to remember as much detail as you can about him and to call them as soon as possible. But an Englishman's home is his castle and not surprisingly many will challenge. If you do so it is important not to go too far. The law on self-defence is actually quite clear. You can use any force which is reasonable to repel your attacker. But any use of force which is unreasonable could result in liability to a criminal assault. Reasonableness is of course the key so every case will turn on its own facts. If armed robbers burst into your home in a flurry of gunfire then it may be that virtually any measures in self-defence would be acceptable.

In a much publicised case, an 82 year old was ordered to pay £4,000 compensation for shooting a burglar who tried to break into his allotment shed. Whilst the sympathy vote clearly went to the old boy, the law was probably correct in bringing a prosecution, if only to lay down guidelines for future victims. In this case the burglar was allegedly only after a few garden tools, but in another, thieves dug up a pensioner's entire crop of potatoes and then replanted the foliage to make it look as though nothing had been taken. The police recommend marking tools in the fight against the menace of the gardens, but where is the line to be drawn? Are gardeners also to be expected to engrave their prize leeks or delphiniums?

If you are defending your property (it is worth bearing in mind that 80% of burglaries occur when nobody is at home), it is enough that you honestly believe that the force used is reasonable, but if you are defending your person honest belief will not save you from prosecution unless the force used is in fact reasonable according to the circumstances. In most cases you would actually be the owner of the property which you seek to protect, but even if not the owner you will not incur any criminal liability if you honestly believe yourself to be the owner. As an example, if you honestly but mistakenly believe that you have a right of way across your neighbour's land and tear down his shed which you consider infringes your right of way, no offence of criminal damage would be committed.

## 9.2 SECURING YOUR HOME

Summer is one of the most popular seasons for thieves. Houses are left empty with curtains drawn. A persistent thief would not take too long to realise that you and your family are off on the annual sojourn. A burglary occurs on average every thirty seconds in the UK and if you live in an inner city location there is a 20% chance that you will be burgled. But the damage can clearly be limited. Most homeowners have very inadequate security. If you cannot put the burglar off altogether, at least make his life difficult. Making your home safe need not cost the earth and indeed many insurers now insist on decent locks and alarms before they offer cover. The market for home security devices is huge and there are many gadgets and systems on the market. Always remember that as most burglaries are opportunist crimes, look for locks etc. which will convince the thief to try your neighbour's house. Buy locks which carry the British Standard and make sure that the hinge side of the door is properly reinforced. If you fail to do this the expense of the good quality locks will have been wasted. Do not neglect the rear or side of your home - these are the most likely targets. Always try to fit locks to ground floor doors and windows but do not leave the keys in an obvious place. Under doormats or plant pots, hanging by a string or a under a window sill are unlikely to prove too much of a challenge to the average burglar! It is worth considering that if an external door is secured properly, and the thief cannot make his escape through it, then he is unlikely to be able to walk away with too much.

The best deterrents are dogs and alarms. For many, keeping a dog is too physically demanding and in any event you would probably have to put your pooch into kennels when you go on holiday. Alarms are very effective, but remember to tell your neighbours to call the police if it goes off. Alternatively you could invest in an alarm which goes straight through to a central monitoring station. A basic system will cost around £500 although the more sensors you require the more expensive it will become. If you cannot afford the annual home contents insurance premium, an alarm system may be something of a luxury. But if you do invest in such preventive measures, make sure it is one approved by the National Approval Council For Security Systems (NACOSS).

An ingenious new device called Smokecloak is also helping the homeowner to fight back. The Smokecloak fills rooms with a harmless glycol mist within twenty seconds of a sensor detecting an intruder. In addition to a basic alarm, timer switches on lights and televisions can prove highly effective. These are relatively inexpensive. Security lights and cameras also offer peace of mind but will be most effective if placed at the rear of the house and not the front as most people think. Finally, your local Crime Prevention Officer will come to your home and offer an array of tips and recommendations. For example he may advise you to plant prickly bushes in the garden at strategic points. He should even be able to give you the details of suitable shrubs and where to get them from. If you are confronted by a burglar, the safest advice is always to give him what he is asking for.

## 9.3  NEIGHBOURHOOD WATCH

The days of twitching net curtains for the sake of neighbourhood gossip have now largely disappeared. Indeed we have probably gone too far the other way - nobody really takes much interest in local affairs and the temptation to look the other way if a crime is being committed is too great for many people. Hopefully the situation will never become as bad as in the USA. Neighbourhood Watch is the acceptable face of community snooping and now has over five million members. Where schemes operate, there is often a noticeable effect on crime in the vicinity. The government is very much in favour of expanding and developing self-policing and has recommended that 130,000 Schemes be allowed to patrol their own streets. A Code of Practice ensures that any such patrols are voluntary and worked out with the police. Members are not required to take direct action if they see a crime but would be expected to call the police immediately.

Private security firms are also expected to take over traditional police duties. Private companies are patrolling streets and housing estates in areas covered by more than 25% of police forces in England and Wales. Fifteen of the forty-three forces in England and Wales currently have private security companies operating private patrols. Some councils have appointed town centre security managers whilst a number of affluent districts are hiring private firms to offer a security service, literally in their own back yards.

The police view such companies with some scepticism but reluctantly accept that given current financial restraints, they are here to stay. Indeed if the American model is considered, then there is clearly scope for the continued development of the private security firm. But remember that such firms' employees have no more power than any other member of the public. Imitating a police officer is also an offence. But a presence of some description is likely to be a deterrent to would-be thieves.

A novel development of this theme is being introduced in some areas. Families in estates are being asked to tune into unused channels on their televisions to spot criminals. Closed circuit cameras are being fed directly into resident's homes and provide a panoramic, twenty-four hour view of the neighbouring area. Talk about big brother! Once the initial fears about prying eyes had dissipated, the service has proved to be of immense success in giving people a degree of control over the villains. The way ahead is clearly a combination of private security firms working in harmony with the police and community as a whole. At present the situation is somewhat haphazard and in need of regulation.

## 9.4  THE POLICE VIEW

The police are aware of the fact that they have to become more accountable to the public which they serve. It would seem that the message of the homeowner as a victim is finally getting through, at least in terms of property crime. The Metropolitan Police has set aside half a million pounds to extend the DNA techniques used so successfully in the fight against violent crimes, to domestic burglaries. This scheme is to work alongside the likes of Operation Bumblebee which has already reduced the number of dwelling house burglaries by 16%. This amounts to around two thousand homes being spared. The Met now rank burglary equally with terrorism and armed crime as the three most important targets. The main bar to bringing more successful prosecutions has traditionally been one of evidence. It is hoped that widespread DNA testing (which can put someone at the scene of a crime from a minute body cell sample) will make it easier to secure convictions.

## 9.5  LIABILITY FOR VISITORS TO YOUR HOME

As far as the law is concerned, as a homeowner you are technically the occupier and potentially liable to any visitors who may have an accident whilst on the premises. In broad terms this applies to any lawful visitor who has a legitimate reason for being on your property. For example, postmen. Although most postmen are pretty hardy souls used to braving all sorts of people and weather, you could be liable if your postie slips on your iced covered path and breaks his ankle. For him to succeed with such a claim, he would have to show that you had been negligent in not clearing away the ice, that an accident was a likely result of your failure to do so and that the damage he suffers is reasonably foreseeable. There may also be the question of contributory negligence - did the postman in some way contribute to his accident ?

If you keep a pet, you could also be liable if they cause damage to person or property. So if your loveable pooch nips the paper boy's hand and causes damage, do not be surprised if you hear from his parents and/or his solicitors. Putting up a sign warning of your dog will probably not suffice. You cannot avoid your liability to someone who has sustained a personal injury through your negligence. In the case of the paper boy, a failure to contain the dog would probably be regarded by a court as negligent.

The position in regard to children wandering onto your land uninvited is interesting. Technically they may have no authority to be there, but the law makes allowances for the adventurous nature of young children. You must therefore take such reasonable precautions as are necessary to prevent children from entering dangerous property. Rubbish heaps, garden sheds and bonfires etc. are all potentially very appealing to the youngster. They are also potentially lethal so you must act reasonably to either secure the allurement or make it as unattractive as possible. Apart from children, you are only liable in negligence to lawful visitors. You would not therefore be liable (even if negligent) to burglars, squatters, tramps and the like. But you cannot abuse this freedom by deliberately laying traps for the unwary trespasser. For example if you set a trap to catch a burglar and he suffers damage, you may well be liable to him for compensation.

If a visitor does have an accident on your premises, their claim will be against you personally. Even relatively minor personal injuries could warrant damages of several thousand pounds. Ouch! With Legal Aid becoming increasingly difficult to obtain, insurance is likely to be your only salvation. When you next renew your contents policy, check whether it offers third party liability cover. If it does, check the extent of the insurance. Some policies offer protection for claims arising out of damage which for example, your dog may have caused by running out into the road and denting an oncoming car. In addition, you may consider taking out additional legal expenses insurance which covers you for lawyers' fees in the pursuit or defence of litigation. Speak with a broker or your direct insurer to ascertain the products currently on the market.

# Chapter 10

## Debt problems - the legal consequences

Lawyers do not make good debt counsellors. This chapter is not intended to offer advice on how to avoid getting into debt or for that matter how to help yourself if financial problems do arise. There are many books far better suited to this role. There are also many advice agencies who can offer expert advice and guidance on dealing with debt. Debt has many consequences - some personal, some individual, some practical and some legal. It is this latter category which will be considered in this chapter.

Debt is a real problem for many members of society. It can strike at the most unexpected of times, often through no fault of the homeowner. Debt does not affect only the less privileged members of the community. In fact many professional, high earning people are often the worst hit. If you earn well, the tendency is to spend well, often beyond your means. If debt strikes, picking yourself up from the fall could be a very long and painful process.

## 10.1  NEGATIVE EQUITY
Negative equity is a particularly nasty form of debt which affects homeowners. If your mortgage is greater than the value of your property, you are in a negative equity situation. This problem has arisen out of the artificially high property prices of the 1980's, so if you are in this net, then it is not your fault. There are estimated to be more than one million homeowners suffering from negative equity. The average size of the problem is £7,000 but it is most acute in the South East where the figure rises to £9,500.

If house prices improve fairly dramatically, then by sitting tight, your problem could disappear. Remember that negative equity is really only a problem if you want to move and you do not possess heavy savings to cover the shortfall. If waiting is not an option because your circumstances have changed, there are schemes available to help the afflicted. Some building societies will allow you to borrow up to around 125% of the purchase price of your new property. This means that you can repay your existing loan in full even though you have not realised enough cash from the sale of your existing property. To be offered such a lifeline, you will need a good track record. You should not have missed any mortgage payments and you definitely should not be in arrears. Some lenders will also permit you to let out your home under an approved tenancy agreement and effectively advance you a second mortgage. But again you would have to prove a reliable track record and show that you have sufficient income to cover the second mortgage.

## 10.2  MORTGAGE ARREARS
Mortgage arrears should not be confused with negative equity. If you are in arrears, it means that there is a shortfall in the mortgage repayments. You

may only be able to afford part of the sum due monthly, or you may simply not be making any payments at all. This is potentially a very worrying time for the homeowner as the lender is quite at liberty to repossess your home. In recent years the number of repossessions has reached a ridiculously high figure. Whilst the rate of repossessions has slowed, if you fall into arrears, do not be surprised if the lender takes a hard line.

Whatever your personal circumstances, you must make contact with the lender. Assistance from trained debt counsellors may go some considerable way in smoothing the path. Do not hand back the keys. Whilst this may seem to be a tempting and easy solution to the problem, your liability to the lender will continue until the property has been formally repossessed and sold on. The interest on the loan will continue to accrue even if you are no longer living in the property. There may also be costs to pay on top of an already spiralling debt.

If you ignore the reminders sent by the lender, within a few months you will be served with a county court summons. This is the first formal stage of repossession proceedings by the lender. Once the hearing date arrives the bank or building society will have to produce evidence to the District Judge to show that you are sufficiently in arrears to have breached a covenant to maintain the repayments. If the court is satisfied, it will grant a possession order in favour of the lender. This means that you will have to leave the property by a set date unless you immediately appeal against the decision. The property will eventually be sold off to pay the mortgage. If the sale of your former home does not raise enough cash to cover the shortfall, you will still be personally liable to the lender concerned. Also the costs of making the sale will be deducted before the balance is applied to paying off the mortgage. This is a dreadful situation to be in, particularly if you are hounded for any shortfall.

If you can produce evidence to show that you are making regular payments, even if a long way short of the agreed sum, or that your personal circumstances have changed or are about to change, then the District Judge will show some leniency. The court is at liberty to suspend the possession order to allow you the opportunity to get back onto an even keel. There may be a return date for another hearing - if by then you can show that you have stuck to the agreement, the court is very unlikely to order possession. The judiciary as a whole has been something of a reluctant player in this massive problem. Judges are really not in the habit of making people homeless unless the circumstances are very dire and you have made no effort to address the situation.

### 10.3   BANKRUPTCY

If your debt problems are very severe, then bankruptcy may be the only answer. But it is a much misunderstood term and the consequences of bankruptcy are far more severe than many people realise. By declaring yourself bankrupt or by being made bankrupt by your creditors does not mean that your debts are magically wiped out. You will have to repay what you can.

### Creditor's petition

If you owe more than £750, one or more of your creditors can ask a court to make you bankrupt. You will be served with a bankruptcy petition and summoned to a court hearing. If the court finds for the creditors, a bankruptcy order is made against you. Most of your property then legally comes under the control of the official receiver. The next stages are as follows:

- statement of affairs.
- official receiver investigates conduct and affairs of the bankrupt.
- creditors' meeting (possibly a Public Examination) to appoint Trustee in Bankruptcy.
- ownership of bankrupt's "available property" vests in the Trustee.
- trustee pays the creditors, usually in instalments.
- final meeting of creditors for discharge of bankrupt (automatic discharge in most cases after three years).

### Debtor's petition

You can also apply to make yourself bankrupt by filing a petition at your local county court. The petition should be accompanied by a fee and a Statement of Affairs (which sets out all your assets and liabilities). The court will normally make an immediate Bankruptcy Order which will be administered summarily by a trustee in bankruptcy. However if your total debts are less than £20,000 and you have assets of less than £2,000, then the court may appoint a licensed insolvency practitioner to consider the situation.

The rationale behind this is to see if voluntary arrangements can be entered into with your creditors. In straightforward cases of self-petition, you will be automatically discharged from bankruptcy after two years. When the period expires, an application should be made for a certificate of discharge from the court. If you have been bankrupt twice in the previous fifteen years, then you must apply for discharge by order of the court. Once discharge is achieved there is generally no obligation to repay any previous debts.

## Consequences of bankruptcy
### Your home
This will usually be the main asset so the trustee may be looking for a quick sale. However if there is a spouse then the trustee cannot obtain possession for at least twelve months after the bankruptcy. But if you live alone or with an unmarried partner, there will be no period of grace. All other assets apart from basic necessities can be seized by the trustee. The trustee can also intercept some of your earnings by asking the court to make an Income Payments order. Such an order would compel your employer to pay some of the wages direct to the trustee.

### Marital breakdown
All too often this rather sad situation follows hot on the heels of a bankruptcy. If you are in financial difficulties and transfer your principal asset, namely the matrimonial home, into your wife's name the court may set aside such a transaction which would clearly be an attempt to defeat your creditors. Also, a bankrupt cannot:

- obtain credit of more than £250 without disclosing that he is an undischarged bankrupt.
- trade under any name other than that name by which he was made bankrupt.
- sit as an MP or member of the House of Lords, or be an estate agent, school governor, solicitor or accountant.
- be a manager or company director without the permission of the court.

A bankrupt may have been found to have committed certain offences prior to or upon bankruptcy by:

- not keeping records in the immediate preceding two years.
- contributing to his insolvency in the immediate preceding two years by gambling cash or hazardous speculations.
- disposing of property by gift unless he can show no intent to defraud.
- leaving or even preparing to leave the country with any property worth more than £500 unless with the consent of the trustee.

## 10.4 ADMINISTRATION ORDERS
These allow you to add all your debts together and make just one payment into the county court each month. The court then distributes the money to

your creditors in proportion to the amount owed to them. To obtain an administration order:

- you must have a court judgment outstanding and have credit debts of less than £5,000 in total.
- all your credit debts in full must be included in the order.
- rent or mortgage arrears from a previous property can be included as can hire purchase debts where the goods have been repossessed/returned.
- priority debts are usually excluded.

Administration orders are beneficial because they allow you to make just one payment which ought to be well within your ability to pay. Also once the order is made no further interest is added to the debt. It does not carry the stigma of bankruptcy. On the negative side, once made, you cannot obtain credit without informing the Lender of the Order. If you do not make the payments under the order you will be left to deal with your creditors individually without the protection of the court.

## *10.5* STATUTORY DEBTS

Statutory debts such as council tax, income tax, national insurance and TV licences are dealt with on an altogether more formal footing in the magistrates' courts. In such cases the court has the power to issue liability orders, warrants for distress, fines and even order imprisonment. On such matters you should seek legal advice from a solicitor - Legal Aid may be available.

## *10.6* VOLUNTARY ARRANGEMENTS

Bankruptcy is a fairly drastic measure for any homeowner to consider. In most cases it should be seen as a last resort. Before you consider such draconian steps, you could put a written proposal to all your creditors asking them to accept some form of arrangement. For example the creditors may agree to accept 50p in the pound of debts owing in full and final settlement. But it would take the agreement of all of them for it to have any binding effect in law. Many creditors are receptive to helping out in genuine cases and will do what they can to accommodate. If they fail to agree then you could approach a licensed insolvency practitioner who can enter into correspondence on your behalf and seek a formal individual voluntary arrangement (IVA). But this procedure is expensive and should be considered carefully to see if it really makes economic sense.

# Chapter 11

## Useful miscellany

## *11.1* COUNCIL TAX

The council tax is payable in respect of dwellings (defined by the General Rate Act of 1967). The following are not regarded as a dwelling unless it forms part of a larger property which is itself a dwelling:

- a yard, garden or outhouse attached to property used wholly as a domestic residence.
- a private garage which either has a floor area not exceeding twenty-five metres or is used wholly or mainly for keeping a private vehicle.
- storage premises used wholly or mainly for the storage of domestic items.

Exempt dwellings fall into three categories:
**Classes A & C** - vacant dwellings. **Classes B, D to L and Q** - unoccupied dwellings. **Classes M to P** - dwellings in these classes can be either occupied or unoccupied.

So the council tax is payable on any dwelling which is not exempt. The person liable to pay the tax is the one with the most senior legal interest:

- the resident who holds the freehold or;
- a resident who has a leasehold interest or;
- a resident who is a statutory or secure tenant or;
- a resident who has a contractual licence to occupy or;
- a resident or;
- the owner of the dwelling.

If there are two or more people on the same level and there is no one higher up, they are each jointly and severally liable to pay the council tax. Only residents over eighteen years of age are required to pay the tax. The tax is assessed according to a series of valuation bands.

| ENGLAND | BAND |
|---|---|
| Houses up to £40,000 | A |
| £40-52,000 | B |
| £52-68,000 | C |
| £68-88,000 | D |
| £88-120,000 | E |
| £120-160,000 | F |
| £160-320,000 | G |
| Over £320,000 | H |

**Table 5. The council tax bands in England.**

| WALES | BAND |
|---|---|
| Houses upto £30,000 | A |
| £30-39,000 | B |
| £39-51,000 | C |
| £51-66,000 | D |
| £66-90,000 | E |
| £90-120,000 | F |
| £120-240,000 | G |
| Over £240,000 | H |

**Table 6. The council tax bands in Wales.**

The amount of tax payable differs in specified proportions according to the valuation band. Property in band A is given the value of 6. A person in band H pays proportionately three times more council tax than a person in band A.

**Example**. If a council sets a tax for band D of £623, and your property is in a different band, you will pay:

| BAND | PROPORTION | TAX PAYABLE (£) |
|---|---|---|
| A | 6 | 415 |
| B | 7 | 484 |
| C | 8 | 554 |
| D | 9 | 623 |
| E | 11 | 761 |
| F | 13 | 900 |
| G | 15 | 1038 |
| H | 18 | 1246 |

**Table 7. Example of council tax payable.**

**Discounts**

Residents may be entitled to a discount of 25% or 50% according to their status. Reductions can also be applied for by those suffering from prescribed disabilities.

## Granny flats

The High Court has ruled that families who have "granny flats" attached to their homes, so that they can look after elderly relatives, must pay two lots of council tax.

## Appeals

If you think that your property has been incorrectly valued or has been wrongly classified, you can appeal to a valuation tribunal. Before you appeal, you must serve a written notice on the billing authority stating the grounds upon which the appeal will be based. The billing authority is bound by law to consider your grievance but need not do anything. If this is the case, then two months after your written notice has expired and within a further two month period, a full-blown appeal can be made to the valuation tribunal. A notice of appeal is sent to the clerk of the tribunal for the area in which your home is situated. The notice must contain:

- grounds of appeal.
- the date of the written complaint to the billing authority.
- the date of any notification received from the billing authority.

An appeal on the basis that the original valuation of your property was incorrect can now only be made if you become the taxpayer for the first time in respect of the property during the period of the valuation list or the property is first entered on the list. Such an appeal is made by lodging an appeal with the local Valuation Office Agency. The period for appeal is six months from the relevant date and in all cases council tax remains payable whilst an appeal is pending.

## 11.2 TIMESHARE

It is estimated that 300,000 Britons own timeshare weeks. In theory the concept of timeshare is sound and well run schemes can be highly attractive. But the industry as a whole has a terrible reputation. Pressure selling and the requirement to part with large sums "up-front" have left many people disgruntled and in debt. Because most timeshare selling is done whilst you are in a relaxed frame of mind whilst on holiday, buying into a dream can prove to be just too much of a temptation for many people. Human nature. Although research suggests that 75% of owners are satisfied with their purchase, the 25% of owners who are less than satisfied can find themselves in big trouble. Buying tips:

- never be tempted into attending presentations on the promise of a fantastic gift or holiday.

- always, always, always sleep on your decision - do not be rushed into signing the agreement.
- be wary of paying a deposit by credit card - the payment cannot subsequently be stopped, unlike a cheque.
- Spain has no cooling-off period to allow you the chance to change your mind. It will not have one until 1997 when EU rules force countries to follow the example already set by Britain and Portugal.
- if possible, try to buy into a development which is a member of the Timeshare Council (see Useful Addresses). All Timeshare Council members are committed to provide high standards of service and integrity in dealing with their customers. In particular they must operate within The Council's Code of Conduct. This includes provisions to ensure that buyers have secure occupancy rights and satisfactory arrangements are in force to protect any monies invested prior to completion of the development. Importantly the Timeshare Council also operates a free advisory and conciliation service for purchasers who are in dispute with its members. Unfortunately, many developers are not members of the Council. If you have to resell your timeshare, then making sure that the developer is a Council member is even more critical because of the number of crooks operating in the market. There are seven resale agencies which are members. The Council demands that they present the business history of the directors, an audited history of at least fifty resales and one year's trading before allowing them to become members. They must also offer a fourteen day cooling-off period (not a legal requirement).
- enlist the help of a lawyer if you are in any doubt.

## 11.3 A SECOND HOME

For many people the dream of owning a second or holiday home can easily become a reality. But all the problems associated with one home will at least double if you venture into the property market again. In fact all the potential neighbour disputes or frozen pipes during the winter etc. which may occur when you are not at home can be much more difficult to deal with by remote control. That said, the principal differences in owning a second home relate to money. You are not entitled to any income tax relief on the interest you pay under a mortgage. You cannot say that you and your partner own a different home and claim relief on two mortgages.

If you sell a second home at a profit, then unlike your principal home, you will be liable to capital gains tax (CGT) on the "profit". But the cost of improvements which increase the value of the home can be added to the original cost price when calculating the tax due after sale. This has the effect of reducing the profit and therefore your liability to CGT. In terms of property insurance, do not be surprised if policies seem very expensive. Insurers tend to view second homes as being a greater risk simply because they may be left unoccupied for long periods. Second homes will be the subject of a claim for council tax just like your main residence. The only way that the property may be regarded as exempt is if it falls into Class C i.e. an unoccupied and substantially unfurnished dwelling.

## 11.4 TELEVISION LICENCES

All TV sets capable of receiving broadcasts must be licensed. One licence covers all the sets used in one household but if you live in rented accommodation, it is your responsibility to obtain a licence, even if the TV is provided by the landlord. The penalty for not holding a valid licence could be a very painful fine of up to £1000.

## 11.5 RAFFLING YOUR HOME

Desperate times call for desperate measures. Some people have tried raffling their homes to beat the slump in the property market. If enough tickets are sold, the anticipated sale price should be reached or even exceeded. But such raffles or lotteries in which there is no element of competition, but are pure chance, are illegal. Although prosecutions are rare you should be very wary of conducting such an event.

## 11.6 BLIGHT

In general, blight refers to the depressing effect on property values of public sector road or building developments. For example, your property would be "blighted" if a new six lane motorway passed at the bottom of your garden. Not only would its value plummet but it would be virtually impossible to sell. In the most extreme cases, the government, or one of its appointed agencies, would compulsorily purchase adjoining property. In other cases you would be entitled to compensation for a diminution in value of your home under the Land Compensation Act 1973. The detail involved is too much to consider here, but there are strict statutory controls to protect homeowners who are affected by such public sector developments. In the private sector, the situation is different. If one of the large retailers builds a new superstore near to your home, you have no absolute right to claim the same compensation as if you were faced with public sector development. But the retailer concerned would be anxious not to make waves locally which could scupper their planning application. It is usual for sweeteners to be offered - financial compensation or an agreement to develop local civic amenities. Perhaps a re-landscaping programme or a sponsored community centre etc. If you are in doubt contact the Royal Town Planning Institute (see Useful Addresses).

## 11.7 SQUATTERS

If someone gains entry to your home without your consent and without having forced their way in, then they are termed a squatter. Evicting squatters was traditionally a difficult and in some cases, complex procedure, particularly if violence was involved. Now, the Criminal Justice and Public Order Act 1994 allows homeowners to go to court without notifying the squatter, for an "interim possession order" of the property. Thereafter the squatters must leave within twenty-four hours, failing which they can be sent to prison for up to six months. A constable in uniform may arrest the squatters if they fail to leave. The squatters have to leave, even if they intend later to claim a right of occupation. However, in such a case they may have the right to be restored to occupation and to compensation.

## 11.8 BAILIFFS

If you do find yourself on the wrong end of a county court judgment or a magistrates' court liability order (unpaid Council Tax), the creditor may send round the bailiffs in order to seize possession of some of your goods to the value of the debt. The goods are eventually sold at auction and the proceeds will also be used to cover the bailiff's fees. But, contrary to popular belief, bailiffs do not have the right to break down external doors or force entry. They can gain entry through an open door or window, but otherwise can only come into your home at your invitation. Bailiffs cannot enter premises on a Sunday but they can break down internal doors once inside, if necessary. They cannot seize:

- items necessary for personal use in your job - tools, books etc.
- items necessary for satisfying your basic domestic needs - clothing, bedding, furniture etc.
- items belonging to someone else, for example your spouse or goods which are on hire purchase.

# Glossary of terms

**Ancient lights**. Windows which have had uninterrupted light for at least twenty years.

**Bailiff**. A court officer appointed to issue and execute legal documents and processes.

**Bankruptcy**. When a court takes over a debtor's assets on behalf of his creditors.

**Centralised lender**. A relatively new type of lender which operates from a single central office. Centralised lenders obtain their lending money from the international money markets.

**Clear-up rates**. This is a statistic which the police use to gauge how many crimes are being solved. Primary clear-ups are offences deemed to be cleared up by means of a charge, summons or caution - not in terms of successful convictions.

**Creditor**. A person owed money.

**Compulsory first registration of title**. Under the "new" system of property transfer, all homes will eventually be registered at the land registry. Homes which have previously been unregistered will have to be on the next sale or death of the owner.

**Constructive notice**. This is a term applied to certain types of property transaction. Constructive notice is where knowledge of a fact is presumed by law.

**Conveyancing**. A general term used to describe the whole procedure for buying and selling freehold and leasehold property.

**Curtilage**. The garden or other piece of land which surrounds and is owned by the homeowner.

**Deed**. A formal legal document, most often used in property transactions.

**De Minimis**. Of such minor significance that the law need not become involved.

**Defendant**. The person (or company) against whom legal proceedings are brought.

**Dominant tenement**. The land which has the benefit of an easement.

**Easement**. A right enjoyed by the owner of land, such as a right to light, over the land of another person.

**Enforcement notice**. A type of notice, issued usually by the local authority, preventing someone or a firm from committing a civil wrong.

**Enfranchisement**. The process whereby a group of flat owners can buy the freehold to their properties.

**Environmental health officer**. Employed by the local authority to enforce laws which protect our local environment, such as noise and pests.

**Equitable interest**. A right which a person may acquire in a property, not laid down in writing, but which would be unfair if it were not protected.

**Equity**. The amount by which the sale (or value) of your home exceeds the mortgage or other charge on it, once paid off. For example, if your mortgage is £50,000 and your home is valued at £75,000, the equity in it is said to be £25,000.

**Freehold**. A form of owning land where ownership is unlimited, i.e. you own the land outright forever.

**Garnishee proceedings**. A means of enforcing a court judgment whereby the debtor's bank account can be ordered to pay any incoming sums to the plaintiff.

**General development order**. A piece of legislation which allows certain property developments without the need to obtain planning permission.

**Housing Association.** A group of people can register themselves as a housing association with a view to constructing new homes or converting old ones. If the government approves the scheme it will finance the building works through grants from the Housing Corporation.

**Indemnity cover.** A type of insurance whereby the age and wear of your lost or damaged items is taken into account by the insurance company.

**Injunction.** A court order requiring someone to do something (mandatory) or more usually to prevent them from doing a specified thing.

**Intentionally homeless.** You cannot apply successfully for council housing if you leave your last established accommodation through deliberate actions or neglect. An example of intentional homelessness is a persistent refusal to pay rent or mortgage even though funds permit.

**Joint tenancy.** A form of multiple property ownership where on the death of one of the joint tenants, his share transfers automatically to the surviving joint tenants. You cannot leave your share to someone else under a will where a joint tenancy is in existence.

**Judgment in default.** A type of final judgment in civil proceedings which the plaintiff can apply for if the defendant fails to carry out one of the procedural requirements, for example failing to file a defence on time.

**Land registry.** The government body responsible for registering all land.

**Land registry certificate.** In effect this is the title deed which shows who owns the land. If the property had previously been unregistered the buyer's solicitor will look to the old deeds.

**Lands tribunal.** The place in London where certain disputes over land ownership are fought out.

**Lay representative.** A non-lawyer who is entitled to conduct litigation on your behalf.

**Leasehold.** A type of land ownership which is less than a freehold, usually for a fixed number of years.

**Legal charge**. A type of security which a lender has over your property. A mortgage is a legal charge which will stay on the register until the mortgage has been paid off (redeemed).

**Licensed conveyancer**. An alternative to using a solicitor for your conveyancing needs. Licensed conveyancers are not qualified lawyers but have considerable experience of buying and selling property.

**Liquidated damages**. A specific sum which can be calculated as owing to a plaintiff.

**LPA**. Local Planning Authority.

**Local search**. One of the preliminary stages of a conveyancing transaction. Your solicitor will carry out a search at the local authority to see if there are any development plans etc. which may affect your proposed new home.

**Mesne profits**. Rents or profits accruing during the rightful owner's exclusion from his property.

**Miras (Mortgage Interest Relief at Source)**. The amount of income tax relief you are allowed by virtue of having a mortgage. Miras is only available per household and not to each joint owner. If you have a second home it is not permitted.

**Minor interest**. An interest in registered land which will bind purchasers only if registered on the title register.

**Mitigation of loss**. If you sustain a loss of some description and are claiming against someone for that loss, you are required to go to reasonable lengths to minimise it. For example if you sustain a serious flood which makes your home uninhabitable for a few days, checking in to the nearest five star hotel would not be evidence of you mitigating the loss.

**Mortgage**. A loan of money on the security of a property. The lender is called the **mortgagee** and the borrower the **mortgagor**.

**Mortgage indemnity guarantee**. An insurance policy taken out by the borrower on the insistence of the lender to cover any shortfall between the value of the mortgage and the sale price.

**Negative equity**. Where the amount you owe by way of mortgage exceeds the value of your home.

**New for old**. A type of insurance cover which replaces stolen or damaged items with comparable new ones.

**Noise abatement notice**. One of the steps which can be taken against noisy neighbours. It is usually served by Environmental Health Officers.

**Overriding interests**. Those interests in property which are not registered anywhere but which may nevertheless take effect against the landowner.

**Plaintiff**. The person who brings legal proceedings/who is asserting his legal rights.

**Periodic tenancy**. A tenancy which is for an unfixed period. The tenant pays rent periodically until notice is given by either party.

**Pleadings**. The formal legal documents exchanged between parties to civil litigation which basically state each other's case. Material facts and not the law should be pleaded.

**Prescriptive rights**. A way of acquiring rights over someone else's land by the passage of time. For example, rights to light may be acquired after twenty years.

**Private nuisance**. A type of civil wrong which may be either a disturbance or interference with a person's use or enjoyment of their land or the act of allowing the escape of damaging things such as water, smoke or smells onto another person's land.

**Real property**. The correct legal term for land.

**Registered land**. Land that is registered under the Land Registration Act 1925.

**Repudiation**. The term used by insurance companies when they refuse to admit insurance claims, for example if you have not complied with one of the policy terms.

**Restrictive covenant**. A requirement in a legal document to prevent you from doing something. For example there may be a covenant in your leasehold agreement preventing you from erecting a satellite dish.

**Servient tenement**. The land over which there is an easement.

**Small claims court**. Not a court in itself but an arbitration procedure of the county court to deal with small claims (currently up to £3,000). Lawyers are not encouraged and no legal fees are recoverable - even if you win.

**Stamp duty**. A property tax payable on all purchases of over £60,000.

**Summary judgment**. Judgment which the plaintiff can apply for if the defendant cannot convince the court that he has an arguable case which can form the basis of a defence.

**Tenancy in common**. A form of multiple property ownership whereby each "tenant" holds a clearly identifiable share in the property. Unlike a joint tenancy, tenants in common can leave their share to whomsoever they like under a will.

**Tenure**. The legal term to describe how property is held, for example as leasehold or freehold.

**Title**. The word used to describe legal ownership. If you do not have good title to property, it means that you do not own it.

**Trespass**. A type of civil wrong often misunderstood which means to enter onto somebody's property without their consent. It is not a criminal offence and trespassers cannot be prosecuted.

**Unliquidated damages**. A sum not capable of specific estimation but is at the discretion of the court. Usually claimed in personal injury cases.

**Vendor**. The seller of property.

**Warrant of execution**. A means of enforcing a civil judgment whereby bailiffs are empowered under a warrant to seize the defendant's goods up to the value of the judgment. Eventually the goods may be sold at auction. The bailiff's fees will also be taken from the proceeds.

# Further reading

Pillars of Justice is intended as a practical handbook and as such does not discuss the law in too much detail. There are many good books available if you wish to explore in a little more depth. But be warned, they can be very expensive and cumbersome, even for lawyers. Your local library should have a section devoted entirely to home ownership. Be guided by the staff who should be able to point you in the right direction and avoid an unnecessary waste of time. The following may be worth considering:

Appleby, *A Practical Guide to the Small Claims Court,* (Tolley Publishing)

Lowe and Woodroffe, *Consumer Law And Practice,* (Sweet and Maxwell)

Megarry and Wade, *The Law Of Real Property,* (Stevens)

Pritchard, *The New Penguin Guide To The Law,* (Penguin Books)

Pugh -Smith, *Neighbours And The Law,* (Sweet and Maxwell)

Rogers, *Winfield And Jolowicz On Tort,* (Sweet and Maxwell)

Smith and Bailey, *The Modern English Legal System,* (Sweet and Maxwell)

Williams and Hepple, *Foundations Of The Law Of Tort,* (Butterworths)

# Useful addresses

## Chapter 1 - The legal aspects of property ownership

District Land Registries:

**BIRKENHEAD**
The Birkenhead District Land Registry
Old Market House
Hamilton Street
Birkenhead
Merseyside L41 5FL
Tel: 0151 473 1110

**COVENTRY**
The Coventry District Land Registry
Greyfriars Business Centre
2 Eaton Road
Coventry CV1 2SD
Tel: 01203 860860

**CROYDON**
The Croydon District Land Registry
Sunley House
Bedford Park
Croydon CR9 3LE
Tel: 0181 781 9100

**DURHAM**
The Durham District Land Registry
Southfield House
Southfield Way
Durham DH1 5TR
Tel: 0191 3013500

**GLOUCESTER**
The Gloucester District Land Registry

Bruton Way
Gloucester GL1 1DQ
Tel: 01452 511111

## HARROW
The Harrow District Land Registry
Lyon House
Lyon Road
Harrow
Middlesex HA1 2EU
Tel: 0181 427 8811

## KINGSTON UPON HULL
The Kingston upon Hull District Land Registry
Earle House
Portland Street
Kingston upon Hull
Humberside HU2 8JN
Tel: 01482 223244

## LEICESTER
The Leicester District Land Registry
Thames Tower
99 Burleys Way
Leicester LE1 3UB
Tel: 0116 2654000

## LYTHAM
The Lytham District Land Registry
Birkenhead House
East Beach
Lytham St Annes
Lancs FY8 5AB
Tel: 01253 849849

## NOTTINGHAM
The Nottingham District Land Registry
Chalfont Drive
Nottingham NG8 3RN
Tel: 0115 9351166

**PETERBOROUGH**
The Peterborough District Land Registry
Touthill Close
City Road
Peterborough PE1 1XN
Tel: 01733 555666

**PLYMOUTH**
The Plymouth District Land Registry
Plumer House
Tailyour Road
Crownhill
Plymouth PL6 5HY
Tel: 01752 701234

**PORTSMOUTH**
The Portsmouth District Land Registry
St Andrew's Court
St Michael's Road
Portsmouth
Hampshire PO1 2JH
Tel: 01705 865022

**STEVENAGE**
The Stevenage District Land Registry
Brickdale House
Swingate
Stevenage
Herts SG1 1XG
Tel: 01438 788888

**SWANSEA**
The Swansea District Land Registry
Ty Bryn Glas
High Street
Swansea SA1 1PW
Tel: 01792 458877

**TELFORD**
The Telford District Land Registry
Parkside Court

Hall Park Way
TELFORD TF3 4LR
Tel: 01952 290355

**TUNBRIDGE WELLS**
The Tunbridge Wells District Land Registry
Tunbridge Wells
Kent TN2 5AQ
Tel: 01892 510015

**WEYMOUTH**
The Weymouth District Land Registry
1 Cumberland Drive
Weymouth
Dorset DT4 9TT
Tel: 01305 776161

**YORK**
The York District Land Registry
James House
James Street
York YO1 3YZ
Tel: 01904 450000

Land Charges Department
Drakes Hill Court
Burrington Way
Plymouth PL5 3LP
Tel: 01752 779831
Telephone search service - 01752 701171

Lands Tribunal
48-49 Chancery Lane
London WC2A 1JR
Tel: 0171 936 7200

Royal Institution of Chartered Surveyors
12 Great George Street
London SW1P 3AD
Tel: 0171 222 7000

Leasehold Valuation Tribunal
Newlands House
37-40 Berners Street
London W1P 4BP
Tel: 0171 580 2000

## Chapter 2 - Buying a house (and selling!)

Incorporated Society of Valuers and Auctioneers
3 Cadogan Gate
London SW1X 0AS
Tel: 0171 235 2282

National Association of Estate Agents
Arbon House
21 Jury Street
Warwick CV34 4EH
01926 496800

Office of the Ombudsman for Corporate Estate Agents
P O Box 1114
Salisbury
Wiltshire SP1 1YQ
Tel: 01722 333306

Royal Institution of Chartered Surveyors
12 Great George Street
London SW1P 3AD
Tel: 0171 222 7000

National House Building Council (NHBC)
Buildmark House
Chiltern Avenue
Amersham
Bucks HP6 5AP
Tel: 01494 434477

British Association of Removers
3 Churchill Court
58 Station Road
North Harrow

Middlesex HA2 7SA
Tel: 0181 861 3331

Law Society of England And Wales
113 Chancery Lane
London WC2A 1PL
Tel: 0171 242 1222
    01926 822007 (Helpline)

Law Society of Scotland
26 Drumsheugh Gardens
Edinburgh EH3 7YR
Tel: 0131 226 7411

Solicitors Complaints Bureau
Victoria Court
8 Dormer Place
Leamington Spa
Warwickshire CV32 5AE
Tel: 01926 820082

Office of Fair Trading
Field House
15-25 Bream's Buildings
London EC4A 1PR
Tel: 0171 242 2858

Personal Investment Authority
Consumer Help Desk
Hertsmere House
Hertsmere Road
London E14 4AB
Tel: 0171 538 8860

## Chapter 3 - Insurance

Royal Institution of Chartered Surveyors
12 Great George Street
Parliament Square
London SW1P 3AD
Tel: 0171 222 7000

Association of British Insurers
51-55 Gresham Street
London EC2V 7HQ
Tel: 0171 600 3333

British Insurance and Investment Brokers Association
BIIBA House
14 Bevis Marks
London EC3A 7NT
Tel: 0171 623 9043

Institute of Public Loss Assessors
14 Red Lion Street
Chesham
Buckinghamshire HP5 1HB
Tel: 01494 782342

Insurance Ombudsman Bureau
135 Park Street
London SE1 9EA
Tel: 0171 928 7600

Personal Insurance Arbritration Service
24 Angel Gate
City Road
London EC1V 2RS
Tel: 0171 837 4483

## Chapter 4 - Building, improving, extending your property

Department of the Environment
2 Marsham Street
London SW1P 3EB
Tel: 0171 276 0900

Royal Institute of British Architects
66 Portland Place
London WC1N 4AD
Tel: 0171 580 5533

Local Planning Authority
Contact your local council.

Commission for Local Administration
21 Queen Anne's Gate
London
SW1H 9HU
Tel: 0171 222 5622

Royal Town Planning Institute
26 Portland Place
London WC1N 4BG
Tel: 0171 636 9107

# Chapter 5 - Dealing with the utility companies

Office of Telecommunications (Oftel)
50 Ludgate Hill
London EC4M 7JJ
Tel: 0171 634 8700

Office of Water Services (Ofwat)
Centre City Tower
7 Hill Street
Birmingham B5 4UA
Tel: 0121 625 1300

**Ofwat CSC's:**

Ofwat Central CSC
1st Floor, 77 Paradise Circus
Queensway
Birmingham B1 2DZ
Tel: 0121 212 5202

Ofwat Eastern CSC
Ground Floor, Carlyle House
Carlyle Road
Cambridge CB4 3DN
Tel: 01223 323889

Ofwat Northumbria CSC
2nd Floor, 35 Nelson Street
Newcastle NE1 5AN
Tel: 0191 221 0646

Ofwat North West CSC
1st Floor, Boulton House
17-21 Chorlton Street
Manchester M1 3HY
Tel: 0161 236 6112

Ofwat Southern CSC
3rd Floor
15-17 Ridgmount Street
London WC1E 7AH
Tel: 0171 636 3656

Ofwat South West CSC
1st Floor, Broadwalk House
Southernhay West
Exeter EX1 1TS
Tel: 01392 428028

Ofwat Thames CSC
2nd Floor
15-17 Ridgmount Street
London WC1E 7AH
Tel: 0171 636 3656

Ofwat CSC for Wales
Room 140, Caradog House
1-6 St Andrew's Place
Cardiff CF1 3BE
Tel: 01222 239852

Ofwat Wessex CSC
Unit 2, The Hide Market
West Street
St Philips
Bristol BS2 0BH
Tel: 0117 9557001

Ofwat Yorkshire CSC
10th Floor, Dudley House
Upper Albion Street
Leeds LS2 8PN
Tel: 0113 2340874

*Office of Electricity Regulation (OFFER)*
**Offer Regional offices:**

Eastern Region
4th Floor
Waveney House
Handford Road
Ipswich
Suffolk IP1 2BJ
Tel: 01473 216101

East Midlands Region
Suite 3C
Langford House
40 Friar Lane
Nottingham NG1 6DQ
Tel: 0115 9508738

London Region
11 Belgrave Road
London SW1V 1RB
Tel: 0171 233 6366

Merseyside and North Wales Region
4th Floor
Hamilton House
Hamilton Place
Chester CH1 2BH
Tel: 01244 320849

Midlands Region
Hagley House
Hagley Road
Birmingham B16 8QG
Tel: 0121 456 4424

North Eastern Region
1st Floor
St Cuthbert Chambers
35 Nelson Street
Newcastle Upon Tyne NE1 5AN
Tel: 0191 21 2071

North Scotland Region
24 Marshall Place
Perth PH2 8AG
Tel: 01738 636669

North Western Region
1st Floor Boulton House
17-21 Chorlton Street
Manchester M1 3HY
Tel: 0161 236 3484

South Eastern Region
1-4 Lambert's Yard
Tonbridge
Kent TN9 1ER
Tel: 01732 351356

Southern Region
30-31 Friar Street
Reading
Berkshire TG1 1DX
Tel: 01734 560211

Southern Scotland Region
48 Vincent Street
Glasgow G2 5TS
Tel: 0141 248 5588

South Wales Region
5th Floor
St David's House (West Wing)
Wood Street
Cardiff CF1 1ES
Tel: 01222 228388

South Western Region
Unit 1
Hide Market
West Street
Bristol BS2 0BH
Tel: 0117 9540934

Yorkshire Region
4th Floor
Fairfax House
Merrion Street
Leeds LS2 8JU
Tel: 0113 2341866

The Office of Gas Supply (Ofgas)
Stockley House
130 Wilton Road
London SW1V 1LQ
Tel: 0171 828 0898

## Gas Consumers Council (regional offices)

Scotland
86 George Street
Edinburgh EH2 3BU
Tel: 0131 226 6523

Wales
Caradog House
St Andrew's Place
Cardiff CF1 3BE
Tel: 01222 226547

Northern
Plummer House
Market Street East
Newcastle-upon-Tyne
NE1 6NF
Tel: 0191 261 9561

North East
3rd Floor
National Deposit House
1 Eastgate
Leeds LS2 7RL
Tel: 0113 2439961

North West
Boulton House
Chorlton Street
Manchester M1 3HY
Tel: 0161 236 1926

East Midlands
Pennine House
31-33 Millstone Lane
Leicester LE1 5JN
Tel: 0116 2536633

West Midlands
Broadway House
60 Calthorpe Rod
Birmingham B15 1TH
Tel: 0121 454 5510

Eastern
51 Station Road
Letchworth
Herts GS6 3BQ
Tel: 01462 685399

North Thames
6th Floor
Abford House
15 Wilton Road
London SW1V 1LT
Tel: 0171 931 9151

Southern
3rd Floor
Roddis House

4-12 Old Christchurch Road
Bournemouth BH1 1LG
Tel: 01202 556654

South East
6th Floor
Abford House
15 Wilton Road
London SW1V 1LT
Tel: 0171 931 9151

South West
3rd Floor
Prudential Building
115 Armada Way
Plymouth PL1 1HP
Tel: 01752 667707

## Chapter 6 - Letting out your home

Association of Residential Letting Agents
Maple House
53-55 Woodside Road
Amersham
Buckinghamshire HP6 6AA
Tel: 01494 431680

London Stamp Office
SW Wing Bush House
The Strand
London WC2B 4QN
Tel: 0171 438 7452/7314

## Chapter 7 - Dealing with the neighbours

Land Registries - see Chapter 1

Environmental Health Officers
Contact your local council

Mediation UK
82a Gloucester Road
Bishopston
Bristol BS7 8BN
Tel: 0117 9241234

# Chapter 8 - Dealing with tradesmen/consumer law generally

Federation of Master Builders
14-15 Great James Street
London WC1N 3DP
Tel: 0171 242 7583

National Federation of Roofing Contractors
24 Weymouth Street
London W1N 3FA
Tel: 0171 436 0387

British Carpet Technical Centre
Wira House, West Park Ring Road
Leeds LS16 6QL
Tel: 0113 2591999

Textile Services Association
7 Churchill Court
58 Station Road
N Harrow
Middlesex HA2 7SA
Tel: 0181 863 7755

Glass and Glazing Federation
44-48 Borough High Street
London SE1 1XB
Tel: 0171 403 7177

Institute of Plumbing
64 Station Lane
Hornchurch
Essex RM12 6NB
Tel: 01708 472791

Radio, Electrical and Television Retailers' Association Ltd
Retra House
St John's Terrace
1 Ampthill Street
Bedford MK42 9EY
Tel: 01234 269110

British Carpet Manufacturers Association
Royalty House
72 Dean Street
London W1V 5HB
Tel: 0171 734 9858

British Furniture Manufacturers Federation
30 Harcourt Street
London W1H 2AA
Tel: 0171 724 0854

Council for Registered Gas Installers (Corgi)
4 Elmwood
Chineham Business Park
Basingstoke
Hampshire RG24 8WG
Tel: 01256 708133

National Association of Plumbing,
Heating and Mechanical Services Contractors
14/15 Ensign House, Ensign Business Centre
Westwood Way
Coventry CV4 8JA
Tel: 01203 470626

Companies House
Crown Way
Cardiff CF4 3UZ
Tel: 01222 380801

Mail Order Protection Scheme (MOPS)
16 Tooks Court
London EC4A 1LS
Tel: 0171 405 6806

Centre of Dispute Resolution
100 Fetter Lane
London EC4A 1DD
Tel: 0171 430 1852

Chartered Institute of Arbitrators
24 Angel Gate
City Road
London EC1V 2RS
Tel: 0171 837 4483

Registry Trust Ltd
173/5 Cleveland Street
London W1
Tel: 0171 380 0133

# Chapter 9 - Home security

Crime Prevention Officers
Contact your local police station.

# Chapter 10 - Debt problems - the legal consequences

The Bankruptcy Association of Great Britain and Ireland
4 Johnson Close
Abraham Heights
Lancaster LA1 5EU
Tel: 01524 64305

National Association of Citizens' Advice Bureaux
115-123 Pentonville Road
London N1 9LZ
Tel: 0171 833 2181

# Chapter 11 - Useful miscellany

The Timeshare Council
23 Buckingham Gate
London SW1E 6LB
Tel: 0171 821 8845

# Appendices
## APPENDIX 1 - DRAFT PARTICULARS OF CLAIM

IN THE PILLARS OF JUSTICE
COUNTY COURT                                          Case No. 4764/96

B E T W E E N:                  Andrew Litigator          **Plaintiff**
                                     *and*
                                R D Leakey (a firm)       **Defendant**

-------------------------------------------------------------

### PARTICULARS OF CLAIM

1. The defendant offers plumbing services. On the 1st and 15th June 1995 the defendant attempted to repair a shower at the home of the plaintiff.

2. By virtue of the negligence of the defendant, the plaintiff has suffered loss.

### PARTICULARS OF NEGLIGENCE

i)       Failure to isolate the water supply
ii)      Failure to take any or adequate precautions against flooding
iii)     Failure to fit the correct replacement parts

4.       By reason of the matters aforesaid, the plaintiff has suffered loss

### PARTICULARS OF LOSS

i)       Flooded bathroom carpet                              £200
ii)      Fees of Pro-Plumbers                                 £176.42
                                                              --------
                                                              £376.42

AND The Plaintiff claims damages.

Signed:

Dated:

TO THE District Judge and to the Defendant
*send the original plus one copy to the court together with the issue fee (minimum £10 then 10 per cent of the value of the claim upto a maximum of £65)).*

## APPENDIX 2 - CRIMINAL OFFENCES - STATISTICS: 1994

**1**. In 1994, 5.3 million offences were recorded by the police in England and Wales. This represented a fall of 5% over the 1993 figure.

**2**. The majority of crimes were property offences which accounted for 4.9 million or 93% of all crime and included 1.3 million burglaries and 1.4 million vehicle crimes.

**3**. There were decreases in all types of property offence except theft from the person and criminal damage.

**4**. Burglaries decreased by 112,000. Residential burglaries fell by 48,000.

**5**. Thefts from the person increased to 51,000.

**6**. Thefts from shops and the theft of pedal cycles both fell for the second year running.

**7**. A total of 1.3 million offences were cleared up.

**8**. The clear-up rate for vehicle crime and non-residential burglaries remains at less than 20 per cent.

# APPENDIX 3 - POPULATION STATISTICS: 1994

| | |
|---|---|
| Population | 56,388,100 |
| Area | 22,835,587 hectares |
| Density | 2.4 persons per hectare |
| Number of households | 21,897,322 |
| Average size | 2.5 persons |
| Owner occupied | 66.3% |
| Rented from council | 21.2% |
| Other rented | 12.5% |
| Households with no car | 33.4% |
| Households with one car | 43.5% |
| Households with 2 or more cars | 23.1% |

| | |
|---|---|
| Total persons (16+) travelling to work (23,940,549) by: | |
| car | 60.8% |
| train | 5.8% |
| bus | 9.9% |
| foot | 11.8% |
| % working outside district of usual residence | 34.8% |
| Persons over 18 in higher education: | |
| male | 15.5% |
| female | 11.6% |

# MORE FROM OTTER PUBLICATIONS.......

As motorists, there is no escaping the fact that we have to be constrained by a legal framework and that every time we venture on to the road we are controlling what is potentially a lethal weapon. *WHEELS OF JUSTICE* (1 899053 02 6, £5.95, 128 pp) also written by *Duncan Callow*, is aimed at all, including the legal profession, who would like to find out more about how they would stand legally in any given motoring situation. The easy to understand style makes it extremely accessible and contains a useful glossary of terms to clearly spell out all the legal jargon used. *WHEELS OF JUSTICE* is intended as a practical handbook and draws upon many of the author's experiences, both professional and personal. Key areas covered include:

- Insurance
- The MOT and vehicle safety
- Accidents and dealing with their aftermath
- Drink driving and related offences
- The major motoring offences
- The court process
- The fixed penalty system and the penalty points system
- Parking offences and wheel clamping
- Basic motorcycle law
- Driving on the continent
- Buying a used car

*"You won't want to miss Wheels of Justice...it covers everything you need to know".* Top Gear Magazine

*'This highly readable law book covers all aspects of driving...useful facts abound".* AutoExpress

*"The driver's bible".* The News of the World

*'I doubt whether you will find a better introduction to the subject....I recommend it most highly".* Learner Driver

We are living in an age when violence against car-drivers and theft from cars is on the increase. *ARRIVE ALIVE* (1 899053 00 X, 96 pp, £4.95) is aimed at all who are concerned about their own personal safety on the road and behind the wheel. This step-by-step, easily understood book, will teach the reader how to keep safe, how to recognise and escape attacks, how to prevent car theft and how to deal with all other problem situations before they become deadly emergencies. The book is completely up-to-date, including information on The Channel Tunnel. It explains all the latest protective devices and teaches the best defensive driving techniques. In addition, detailed aerial-view diagrams illustrate the situations and manoeuvres described.

*Graham Yuill (A.D.I)* is a qualified Department of Transport Driving Instructor who specialises in training other driving instructors and was assigned as personal bodyguard to the Commander of the Ulster Defence Regiment (now renamed the Royal Irish Regiment) for two years.

**"Packed with information on every aspect of safety for motorists, it's essential reading".** *Woman's Own*

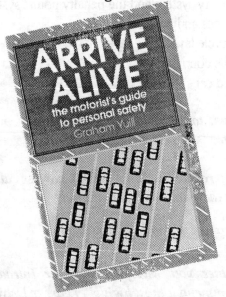

*BEHIND THE WHEEL* (1 899053 01 8, 264 pp, £7.95), also by Graham Yuill, is a step-by-step, highly illustrated handbook for both learner drivers and driving instructors. Now into its third edition, the book has been completely updated and is the **only book to feature detailed computerised diagrams and questions and answers to help the learner driver pass the new theory driving test.** *BEHIND THE WHEEL* will teach the reader all aspects of driving and road safety in 20 easy lessons and is the only book to cover driving instruction for the disabled, the deaf and the unable to speak. The teaching methods used are those laid down by The Department of Transport. A completely up-to-date section on trams has also been included. Finally the events of the driving test day are outlined in full with useful advice and tips.

"Anyone who is learning to drive, or teaching someone else, will appreciate Behind the Wheel". *Woman and Home*

"I would recommend this excellent book to any learner driver. It is invaluable". *Angus Macleod, Sunday Mail. Bank of Scotland Journalist and Reporter of the Year, 1994*

What do you do if you suddenly find yourself thrust into the news or need vital publicity to boost your club, charity or business? Could you cope? Would you know how to ensure that all the coverage was positive and properly targeted? *HITTING THE HEADLINES! : how to get great publicity* (1 899053 05 X, 160 pp, £7.95) takes the stress out of dealing with the press. This invaluable, step-by-step book offers a wealth of easily understood commonsense advice on the best way to get your news into print, how to deal confidently with reporter enquiries and how to maximise the impact of good publicity. Insider tips include:

- The most effective way to approach news editors
- How to place advertising to reach the maximum audience
- How to ensure your press release becomes a headline story
- How to lessen the damage of bad or unwanted publicity

Whether you are a hard-pressed charity fund-raiser, a sports club seeking to raise its profile or a small company wanting to launch its own sales/PR campaign, *HITTING THE HEADLINES* answers all the questions you've ever had about getting great publicity from newspapers, radio stations and TV news services.

*Iain Pattison* has been a journalist for twenty years - as a reporter, feature writer, chief sub editor, journalism teacher, night editor and managing editor on some of the country's top regional newspapers. As well as running evening classes, university workshops and seminars for aspiring writers, he is a media consultant of industry. He holds two national journalism awards.

**How to order:-**
Through your local bookshop or in case of difficulty, please send cheque made payable to Plymbridge Distributors Limited, c Estover Road, Estover, PLYMOUTH, Devon, PL6 7PZ (0175 695745) or your credit card details.